Ethical Cheating:
Exploring the Swinging Lifestyle

Research, Interviews, and Lessons Learned from Thousands of People

By
Dr. Tracy Riley

Licensed Clinical Social Worker
Doctor of Clinical Psychology
Speaker, Author, Mental Health Clinician

Ethical Cheating: Exploring the Swinging Lifestyle
Dr. Tracy Riley

Copyright © 2020
All Rights Reserved.

All right reserved. No part of this publication may be reproduced, distributed, or transmitted in any form or by any means, including photocopying, recording, or other electronic or mechanical methods, without the prior written permission from the author, except in the case of brief quotations embodied in critical reviews and certain other non-commercial uses permitted by copyright law.

First Printing: August 2020

ISBN: 978-1-7354637-0-4

Portions of this book were originally published as What Impact Does Having a Swinging Lifestyle Have on Marital Satisfaction

Dr. Tracy Riley
Tracy Riley Counseling
11555 Central Parkway, Suite 701
Jacksonville, Florida 32224

(904) 704-2527
www.tracyriley.com
www.ethicalcheating.com

Dr. Tracy Riley is available to speak at your business or conference event on a variety of topics. Call (904) 704-2527 for booking information.

Check out her other books: https://www.tracyriley.com/books

Meet Dr. Tracy Riley

Dr. Tracy Riley grew up in Alabama, in a dysfunctional blended family of his, hers, and ours. As the youngest of 10, and after several years of abuse and neglect, she was placed into a group foster home for several years. Her story is one of triumph, overcoming tragedy and finding her way.

Dr. Tracy Riley began her education at Auburn University, obtaining a Bachelor's Degree in Social Work. She moved on to Florida State University, obtaining a Master's Degree, also in Social Work. Shortly thereafter, she became licensed as a Licensed Clinical Social Worker in Florida. Most recently, she obtained her doctorate in Clinical Psychology in 2018 and became licensed in New York.

Dr. Tracy Riley has built her entire career helping individuals, couples and families become the best versions of themselves. She has also worked with other mental health clinicians, sharing her wide knowledge base by teaching clinical skills and business courses.

Her work isn't magic, though the results of her efforts have been magical.

While building a successful business is a great goal to strive toward, Dr. Riley is most proud of her three adult children. Each of them have followed her footsteps in some way, embracing the mental health field.

Are you looking to create your own personal change, grow your business, or improve some aspect of your life?

Would you like to bring Dr. Tracy Riley to your organization or conference as a keynote speaker?

Contact her at (904) 704 2527 or visit www.tracyriley.com

What others are saying about *Ethical Cheating* and Dr. Tracy Riley

There are some things in life you just DON'T discuss. This book goes there, and in great depth and detail. As someone who prefers being in a monogamous relationship, I never really pondered the idea of consensual cheating and I probably never will. However, as a mature woman, who's spent the last 12 years, married to my soulmate, and given the daunting statistics regarding extra marital affairs, I believe this book offers insight on how to keep the love alive, regardless of how you choose to apply it. So far, it's been an eye-opener. To me, it's very refreshing to read a book that is so non-judgmental and allows for all realities to co-exist. I believe it would serve as a tool to enhance our sex life, because the book focuses on honest and clear communication, which is the cornerstone of any successful marriage. Can cheating ever be considered honest? According to this book, it CAN be, given the right set of circumstances which are outlined herein. I believe Dr. Tracy did a fabulous job in providing a manual which breaks down what is usually a very taboo topic. She is going to lead the way to end the inevitable heartache most couples end up facing when they aren't getting their needs met. Bravo!

–Victoria Gallagher, The Law of Attraction Hypnotist

Dr. Tracy Riley is a notable and trustworthy expert in her field. Her Doctoral Thesis was brilliant and the book even better. So much to be learned on what most consider a taboo subject that's always kept in the dark, but now Tracy has brought it into the light!!!

–Michael C. DeSchalit, CH, CLC, CI, Hypnotist - Speaker - Author

There are only two kinds of people: those who admit they've thought about cheating, and those who are lying about it. But now Tracey Riley brings the results of her doctoral research as well as insight gleaned from thousands of client to tell you how it's possible to remain faithful to your spouse AND have glorious extramarital sex! Written with humor and wisdom, this book takes you by the hand and tells you everything you wanted to know about swinging but were afraid to ask.

–James Hazlerig, Harmony Hypnosis

Ding Dong the witch is dead! The wicked witch of condemnation! Let Dr. Tracy Riley open your mind to the real world of love, relationships and sex and discover the secret about the joys of true intimacy.

–Karen Hand, **Hypnotist/Trainer/Author**

Doctor Tracy Riley says it all. Professional credentials and knowledge to deliver the right medicine.

–Rich Guzzi, Life Skills Strategy Coach

Dr. Tracy Riley is a genius in her field of human emotions, interaction and communication at many different levels. Her educational accolades and personal interaction with those from many walks of life, including those in the swinging lifestyle, make her a wealth of knowledge. If you are seeking answers and information without bias from a true tell-it-as-it-is expert, Dr. Riley is certain to deliver.

–Jason Kropidlowski, Professional Hypnotist

Far and away the best introduction to 'the Lifestyle' anyone could ever wish for. Dr. Tracy Riley is at once astute and articulate in describing the allure and benefits of swinging, while also sounding cautionary notes so that whatever a couple does decide to do they are true to themselves. I will be enthusiastically recommending this book to both friends, clients and indeed everyone curious about this oft healthy alternative to monogamy. Truly a brilliant and much needed book.

**–Dr. John H. Edgette, author of "Hypnotic Erotic:
A Practitioners Guide To Sexual Healing"**

As a 25 year veteran firefighter and paramedic with over 15,000 patient contacts, I am keenly aware of the unique skills that one must have to connect with their patient. Dr. Riley's superlative skill set in accomplishing this is something I strive for daily.

–Derrick Dorsey, Retired Paramedic and Hypnotist

Tracy Riley in bringing us her book, *Ethical Cheating*, has pulled back the covers on a topic that has been given lip service without real examination. Many of my own clients seek help with the sexual dysfunctions that are often the result of trauma from bad relationships or ingrained beliefs and their own shame. This is the time and this is the book to start a frank and truthful discussion about the true sexual revolution, about changing rules, boundaries and consent and exploring them. These are especially important for the "vanilla" world to hear. Best part is this isn't a discussion from some Nancy at the bank – it is from an expert in her field. Thanks for sharing this you have given me another tool to help my clients come to a fresh understanding.

–Marc Marshall, CPH

Dr. Riley rose above the circumstances of her upbringing and chose a career where she could help people. She has helped countless people in many different ways such as assisting in adoptions, providing counseling, and also helping people lose weight and quit smoking through hypnotherapy. She is one of the most amazing people I have ever met and I am proud to call her my friend.

–Dusty Wilkes, CPA

Table of Contents

Part One
Introduction

Chapter One : Variety is the Spice of Life 1
Chapter Two : Fringe Benefits 12
Interlude : A Brief History of Swinging 23

Part Two
Delving Deeper

Chapter Three : So You're Thinking about Becoming a Swinger 26
Chapter Four : The Number 1 Question. (What's the Difference Between Cheating and Swinging?) 38

Part Three
How to Make it Happen

Chapter Five : How to Get Started as a Swinger 49
Chapter Six : How to Meet Other Swingers 66
Chapter Seven : The Green-Eyed Monster of Jealousy 79
Chapter Eight : Logistics: The Nitty Gritty of Getting Down and Dirty 90

Part Four
A Glimpse into a New World

Chapter Nine : Stories, Experiences, and the Real Dirt 103
Chapter Ten : Wrapping It Up 113

Chapter One
Variety is the Spice of Life

Ding Dong! We're here to fuck.

Have you ever wondered what it might be like to just ring someone's doorbell and start the intimate act of having sex? Whether it's mostly a stranger, or someone you've had conversations with prior to meeting face to face, or even someone you've met many times, it's a common fantasy. Maybe it's time to turn that fantasy into your reality.

"But--but--that's CHEATING!"

Yes, it's Ethical Cheating--known by many other names: consensual non-monogamy, swinging, "the Lifestyle," extra-marital sex.

The very idea that it is cheating--that you're somehow getting away with breaking the rules--to be non-monogamous speaks to assumptions about what marriage is and what a committed relationship means.

Yet those assumptions have been in flux since recorded history began. In some societies, cheating was acknowledged and expected if not wholly approved of, while in other times and places, adultery, when revealed could lead to loss of religion, family, social status, wealth, and possessions.

Dr. Tracy Riley

"But--but--no one does that! It's just not DONE!"

You'd be surprised how mistaken you are; it's far more prevalent than you think. Based on the ever multiplying number of swinger websites, it is apparent that the swinging lifestyle is practiced far more than it is discussed. A simple web search will find that in the U.S. alone, there are over three hundred swinger lifestyle clubs with an estimated three million members.

While our society is structured around monogamy, non-monogamy is the norm. Statistics show that while 90% of people expect monogamy in their relationships, infidelity rates are as high as 70% of all relationships. We expect monogamy, but we can't maintain it; we cheat anyway—whether emotionally, physically, or a combination of the two.

So just who is doing all this swinging?

Before we go any further, set the book aside for a moment and allow yourself to imagine what the typical swinger might look like. Consider height, weight, age, ethnicity, hair, body type. Can you see their clothing? What about income, education, religion? What is their occupation? Their political views?

No matter what image or description you came up with, you are absolutely correct. No matter who you pictured, that person exists, and that person is a swinger. Maybe that person is your neighbor, your coworker, your family member. Maybe that person is you.

Ethical Cheating

People swing in different ways, and no two swingers take exactly the same approach:

> *Jennifer and Paul have been in the Lifestyle for many years. They enjoy getting to know other couples, wining and dining, and spending time as friends first before moving to the bedroom. It almost sounds like what you might do when you first begin dating someone. They like going on vacations with their closest sexual partners. From the outside, it appears that several couples are enjoying leisure time together.*

> *Stephanie and James cannot be bothered with taking the time to get to know someone on a personal level. They look at photos, share a few messages, and have the understanding that they plan to play on the first meeting. It sounds similar to a one night stand: Although it could lead to more, there's no expectation that it will. They feel having to coordinate the schedule of four busy adults is too complicated, so they just enjoy sex with no strings attached*

If all these people are out there "doing it," why haven't you heard about it more?

Sex in general is a taboo, and anything that deviates from societal expectations even more so. Despite a wealth of information being available, we just don't talk about our sex lives, not in polite company, not at the dinner table. Even with media attention, there remains an air of secrecy surrounding the Lifestyle.

Pressure to live up to unspoken monogamous expectations are high. Some people wonder if they are a freak or a weirdo, or maybe even a sexual deviant, for thinking about having sex with multiple partners. Many are afraid to mention it to their partners for fear of being thought "unfaithful." You may have even had these thoughts yourself.

Being honest with yourself is difficult, and considering your own relationship through a swinger lens can cause some scary thoughts. What if my partner likes having sex with someone more than me? What if a relationship develops and my partner leaves me? What if my family or my coworkers find out?

With all the challenges to adopting a non-monogamous lifestyle, you might wonder why people do it at all. Why risk being considered a freak, a "slut," or worse--just for wanting to have sex with multiple partners?

The truth is, having sex is one of the most natural biological things we engage in. According to Abraham Maslow's Hierarchy of Needs, the physiological need for sex ranks in the same category as our need for air, water, food, and shelter.

Sexuality is an essential characteristic of being human, and it has multiple components. Sexuality can include eroticism, pleasure, and intimacy. It can be experienced and communicated in a variety of ways: thoughts, fantasies, desires, and practices. Relationships are not a requirement in order to have sexual needs met.

In fact, some couples find that extra-marital sexual relationships can enhance their own intimacy:

> *Darlene and Ed engaged in the swinging lifestyle due to Ed's medical problems that prevented him from being able to perform sexually. He felt terrible at the thought of denying Darlene the opportunity to fulfill her sexual needs. The Lifestyle became their way to have intimacy with one another, albeit with a third and sometimes fourth person in attendance.*
>
> *Darlene and Ed could have found alternative ways to engage in intimacy. However, engaging in Ethical Cheating allowed them to continue to experience sexual activity together, and Ed felt like he was giving Darlene an opportunity to have something he couldn't personally provide for her.*
>
> *Darlene appreciated the opportunity to explore her sexuality with other men and women. Because Ed was present, they had shared experiences to discuss, reminisce about, and use to plan for future activities.*

In contrast, some find that accepting non-monogamy can cause their relationship to take on a whole new shape:

> Rose shared with me how her husband had been unfaithful after a dozen years of marriage. Once she learned of the infidelity, she was understandably hurt and confused. She used his infidelity as an opportunity to explore her own sexuality—in this case, with the other woman. The three of them began a long term relationship, living together with their children. Many think Rose's husband got really lucky, since he got to have his cake and eat it, too.

That's the beauty of the swinging lifestyle; each person and each couple can decide for themselves how to maneuver through this way of life.

Why would you willingly choose to let your partner have sex with someone else, perhaps while you watched or enjoyed yourself nearby? There's the obvious reason; there are no limits on the number of sexual partners and experiences one can have, and it is a way to fulfill sexual fantasies.

With that being said, many couples have stated it is not the act of sex by itself that causes them to choose the Lifestyle. Rather, it is so much more. We will explore many of those reasons throughout this book, but one common benefit is that it improves the primary relationship.

We now understand that monogamy does not automatically equate to relationship satisfaction. The great fear seems to be that extramarital affairs indicate marital problems; a single secret infidelity can bring an otherwise wonderful monogamous relationship to a grinding halt when it comes to light.

However, when you have consensual non-monogamy, the other partner is aware of the sex outside the marriage. Despite this approach going against sexual exclusivity, outcomes for people in this Lifestyle have consistently been shown to increase overall relationship satisfaction.

I don't know about you, but I can't think of many things more important than having satisfaction in your relationship. Communication is a key component of satisfaction, and consensual non-monogamy requires it. Once you have the open communication and the ability to talk about sex with another person, while your partner watches or has sex nearby with someone else, you can talk to each other about nearly anything.

Why did I write this book, and why are you reading it?

If you are reading this book--and you are--congratulate yourself and be proud! It's perfectly natural to have questions and not know where to go to get them answered. This isn't the easiest conversation for family dinners, work events, or neighborhood hangouts. (How great would it be if it were?) Who do you ask about this topic? Even in today's relatively progressive climate, we still aren't comfortable talking about sex--especially sex outside of a marriage or primary relationship.

Regardless of your reasons for wanting to know more about the Lifestyle, you are not alone. Consider now to be the time to be excited about life, about sex, and about the possibility of discovering your true self, without fear of shame. Perhaps you have wants, needs, and desires that you haven't shared with anyone else. Possibly the thought of sex with strangers is appealing, or maybe you like the idea of having a friend with benefits, in addition to your primary sexual partner.

You could be reading this book to find ways to maintain your conviction and desire to remain monogamous and faithful. Rest assured there is no goal or plan to change your mind on that idea. Non-monogamy is not for everyone, and you can feel comfortable using this book to define your own identity.

Perhaps you have already been wondering what does Ethical Cheating really mean? Ethical Cheating may be a solution to what you have been considering a problem in your life up until now. Chapter 2 will further outline and define what it is as well as how you can best implement tools, techniques, and strategies to improve your life and relationships.

As you implement the ideas in this book, with an emphasis on clear communication with your partner, your relationship will be enhanced. Stick with me here; whether you find another couple to share intimacy with or not, doesn't matter. That's not the goal.

What's most important is that because of the enhanced communication of physical, emotional, and sexual needs with your partner, your relationship will be better.

When you learn to cheat ethically, you'll no longer be isolated in your life; you'll realize you aren't a freak, you aren't a sexual deviant, and you are actually normal. You'll have a better life, recognizing and understanding that you have choices and that you get to define what's normal for you. The only rule is that there are no rules.

Between one and eight million individuals engage in the swinging lifestyle in the United States alone. If that many people are doing it (pun intended), it stands to reason that it fulfills some purpose or function to make it worthwhile for couples.

By working with your partner, to learn how to ethically cheat, you can set aside any negative behaviors you have already been engaging in and move from the fear of discovery into the knowledge and confidence that you and your partner are on the same page.

Why should you listen to me?

You may be wondering how I came to be so knowledgeable about this lifestyle. As a mental health clinician, I have worked with clients in this lifestyle for nearly twenty years. In my private practice, I coach monogamists and non-monogamists alike; because I'm knowledgeable and accepting of clients in the

Dr. Tracy Riley

Lifestyle, I've ended up working with a lot of people who are exploring their desire to swing, or who are encountering speed-bumps on the road to enjoying openness in their marriage. Two years ago, I completed a doctorate in clinical psychology and studied dozens of articles, books, and reports about this lifestyle. As a part of the dissertation process, I interviewed sixty participants and heard their stories, secrets, and wishes for their future endeavors.

What I found is that when couples communicate well, and when they learn how to cheat ethically, they can enhance the quality of their emotional relationships, meet their sexual needs in a way that benefits both members of the relationship, and reveals to them that their "freaky" desires are actually pretty normal.

An Aside: Due to my extensive knowledge, and the research I've done on the topic, many people assume that I am involved in the swinger lifestyle on a personal level. I won't confirm that, because I don't think my personal sex life is of interest to most people. I won't deny it, either, because some will ponder that if I haven't engaged, I couldn't possibly be knowledgeable enough to teach others. So, I allow people to believe what they want about my experience and whether or not I engage in the Lifestyle. Life becomes easier when you let people wonder.

You may be wondering why this books exists. Sadly, there is not nearly enough written about the Lifestyle. Literature published as recently as thirty-five years ago condemned the Lifestyle for a number of reasons: It was thought that swinging was done out of boredom, or to improve sexual performance, or even to advance one's social network. Many people engage in the Lifestyle because they like sex with no strings attached. It's really that simple.

While writing my dissertation, I learned that research on swinging has lagged behind the ever increasing occurrence of consensual non-monogamy. Despite the curiosity and general interest in people, relationships, and oh yes, sex ... people still aren't talking about it, and they aren't writing about it. Unfortunately, stigma and shame have continued to override the sexual freedom that comes with the Lifestyle.

As you read this book, consider yourself to be the open minded creature that you are. This is a unique approach to life, relationships, and of course, sex. There is no right or wrong. Remember, there are no rules. Only guidelines and ultimately, a determination of what works best for you and your partner.

As you flip the next page and begin chapter 2, consider beginning a new chapter in your own life. Ponder an exciting new part of your life, filled with new experiences. Now is the time to explore and experience not only sexual pleasure, but emotional pleasure as well as sexual freedom with your partner or with a new set of friends and relationships. Ever new parameters are manifesting, as you decide how to take control of your life.

Dr. Tracy Riley

Chapter Two
Fringe Benefits

Ethical Cheating--It's an oxymoron for sure. While being ethical is defined as having morals, or conforming to acceptable standards of conduct, cheating is acting dishonestly or in a way to gain an unfair advantage. Can you be both ethical and cheat? Read on and decide for yourself.

So why have I named the book Ethical Cheating and how can we reconcile these two opposite words? *The Ethical Slut* was first written in 1997 and explored polyamory, open relationships, and other adventures. Its primary message addressed how the individual would explore their own sexuality, as well as navigate relationships throughout one's life. The book's title was intentionally provocative, pairing the term "ethical," which is something good people strive to be, with "slut," something that good girls aren't. I chose my title in the same vein for similar reasons.

Ethical Cheating is primarily about the swinging lifestyle, which characteristically includes couples who swap or share partners. While we may overlap into other types of relationships, the swinging lifestyle is the principal focus of this book. The truth is, many people outside of the Lifestyle define swinging as cheating. Participants within the Lifestyle define cheating quite differently from swinging, something we will explore as a major theme of this book.

In fact, I received some negative feedback on the title of this book, for that exact reason. Participants within the Lifestyle do not believe that swinging is cheating. I want to fully state that I am in agreement with their definition of cheating and how it doesn't equate to the Lifestyle. However, the title of the book reflects the tension that is baked into the Lifestyle, and it's a main theme this book explores. In fact, I consider the number one question of the Lifestyle to be: "What is the difference between the Lifestyle and cheating?" Check out Chapter Four for more details.

In a 2013 research study, authors Griffith and Forbes (2013) note a simple definition for swinging:

Swinging is the consensual exchange of marital partners for sexual purposes.

As this definition does not address an ongoing relationship, but merely sexual encounters, it's clear that the purpose can also be to provide marital fulfillment. Of course the primary couple doesn't have to be married in order to engage in the Lifestyle.

The exact definition of swinging may seem at first to be a simple one; however, in reality the true meaning can encompass many definitions. The swinger lifestyle is a subgroup within a larger classification of consensual non-monogamy. So, let's side step for a moment and talk about monogamy.

Dr. Tracy Riley

The idea that lifelong monogamy is the only goal for a successful relationship has been so ingrained into society that the majority of people have consistently operated on this belief without question. The conventional notion of monogamy and this idea of sex with one person "until death parts us" has become strained and is considered a false narrative by many. Why are we being told that by going to the altar, we are getting family, security, and companionship, yet we are giving up sexual joy and freedom?

Sexuality and sexual behavior are essential in order to understand the human experience. There is no denying that humans have a sweet tooth for sex. And traditional marriage is under attack from all sides; it often collapses from within. The divorce rates increase exponentially, with infidelity accounting for up to 90% of the divorces taking place. How many people do you know that have been unfaithful to their partner? Perhaps you have contemplated the idea or even stepped outside of your relationship. If you haven't, there's an excellent chance that someone you know has, even if they don't talk about it or admit to it.

Almost 50% of all women report a decline in their sexual health, as Viagra breaks sales records year after year. Everywhere we explore, we are seeing oxymorons and double standards. We expect monogamy, yet we prefer to discover our sexuality outside of social constructs.

When asked why she got into the swinger lifestyle, Michelle replied:

> *I've had a desire to be with two men at the same time since my early 20's. No partner was willing to help me fulfill this fantasy until recently. It's been everything I dreamed it would be, and I love it.*

So for Michelle and her first encounter of non-monogamy, her partner didn't get a "swap" with another male or female. This is a great example of how even the swinging lifestyle doesn't necessarily include strict rules or guidelines.

Going back to the swinger lifestyle--the definition requires more than a simple lack of monogamy. There are many variations; boundaries are decided upon by the individuals within the union. Consensual non-monogamy is a term coined to define any arrangement in which individuals engage in more than one sexual or romantic relationship at a time. These relationships may have implicit or explicit guidelines to allow permitted sexual activities by one or both partners.

The swinger lifestyle is also a sub-group of open relationships and can include any number of possibilities outside of a monogamous agreement. The swinging lifestyle typically includes the individuals having a primary relationship with one person, while having sexual (but not romantic) encounters outside the primary relationship.

Dr. Tracy Riley

David and Deanna said this:

> *Well, exploration when we first started ... why not? And then, as life and lifestyles of one another emerged, a respect for what the other needs to be "more whole" and accepting those behaviors. In our case, it has drawn us together because the level of trust is much higher. Limitations are set and respecting those limits is a function of trust and integrity and love in many ways.*

The swinger lifestyle has often been misunderstood as being polyamory. However, in polyamory, there are multiple emotional/romantic relationships, which may or may not include sex (but typically will). Those engaged in the polyamory lifestyle see themselves as finding their safe place to include more than one committed relationship. They are not limited to one relationship and feel comfortable having multiple relationships. Again, the rules and boundaries are for each individual person engaged in any particular lifestyle. As the author of *The Ethical Slut* stated: "We don't always know what fits before trying it on."

Polyamorists and swingers are both groups engaged in consensual non-monogamy, but that is typically where the resemblance ends. Though both lifestyles encompass endless variations, depending on the agreements made by the individuals involved, it's possible to make some broad generalizations about the differences:

Ethical Cheating

In general, swingers are couples that meet with other couples for occasional "hook-ups"; the emphasis is on the sex, and participants set out to avoid becoming emotionally attached to the people they get physical with. "One-night stands" are not unusual to swingers.

Polyamorists, in contrast, focus not just on the sex—though they enjoy that, too!—but also on the emotional connection, feeling that it's not strange to fall in love with multiple people. This may take the form of a committed primary relationship in which one or both partners also have long-term committed secondary relationships, often with people who are also in other primary or secondary relationships. Sometimes a primary relationship may include more than two people, leading to a committed threesome (in which all three people are emotionally and sexually committed to one another), a "V" (in which all three are emotionally committed to one another, but two don't have sex with each other, only with the third partner), group marriages, and other arrangements. The key difference is that polyamory embraces both emotional and physical connections outside of monogamy, while swinging focuses on physical connections, avoiding emotional attachment.

Like any two similar groups, swingers and polyamorists don't always get along, but both groups are united by their decision to find their own sexual morality and free themselves of default monogamy.

Dr. Tracy Riley

We are learning and deciding that there are no right or wrong decisions about our choices. Unfortunately, we have all probably been taught that our sexual desires, our bodies, and our sexuality are shameful. Why is that? That could take a whole chapter to work through, and possibly even an entire book. For now, let's focus on the belief system that many people have been taught: sex is for procreation only, it is embarrassing to want sex, and you can only have sex with one person for the rest of your life to be considered "normal".

In relationships where monogamy is expected, but not achieved, we face the classic "chicken-or-egg" dilemma--which came first? Was there cheating because of marital problems, or did marital problems start because someone cheated? Either way, we know infidelity can bring about the end of a seemingly great relationship, or at the very least cause a great deal of turmoil and hardship. As we discussed in chapter 1, up to 70% of marriages include some type of infidelity, and of the divorces taking place, infidelity is the cause 90% of the time.

It's almost a cliché to hear the wife of an unfaithful husband lament: "It's not so much the sex as the lying that really hurts!" Whether that's always a completely honest statement, many people feel violated by the idea that their partner was dishonest, possibly more so than by the thought of their partner "gettin' nasty" with someone else. After all, honest communication is the cornerstone of any good relationship, and both "fidelity" and "faithfulness" originally mean sticking to an agreement, whether that's the implicit monogamy of exclusive dating or the explicit promise to "forsake all others" in the wedding vow.

But what if an explicit agreement includes the option of sex with outsiders? In that case, "infidelity" can return to its original meaning. Extramarital sex is no longer a violation, so long as the individual upholds their agreements, whether that means informing their spouse or avoiding some other mutually-defined transgression.

However, when you have consensual non-monogamy, the other partner is aware of the sex outside the marriage. Despite this lifestyle going against sexual exclusivity, outcomes for people in the Lifestyle have consistently been shown to increase overall relationship satisfaction. The typical swinging arrangement only includes sex outside the primary relationship, and no secondary relationships are considered. Many people describe it as the best of both worlds.

> *Ben said this of himself and his wife: "I have a high sex drive, and my spouse does too. I would rather do it openly than to wonder about an affair behind my back." Frank confided that he and his partner entered the Lifestyle because he felt as though their marriage was in a rut. Once he felt comfortable having the conversation with his wife Elaine, they were able to explore the Why first, and then move on to the How.*

Dr. Tracy Riley

Swinging stands in stark contrast to traditional notions of marriage, which is conventionally the only moral and legal context in which sexual behavior receives acceptance and approval. Fortunately, the meaning of marriage varies widely from person-to-person and culture-to culture, yet most agree that successful sexual functioning in a marriage directly correlates to marital fulfillment and the endurance of the relationship. Sex and intimacy are the hallmarks of a passionate relationship.

Understanding that monogamy does not automatically equate to relationship success and examining the taboo phenomenon that causes monogamy to be considered the ideal goal of a relationship will help to dispel the myths about the Lifestyle. Research on swinging has lagged behind the increasing occurrence of swinging. There is little research, beyond anecdotal evidence, conducted to determine the marital and sexual satisfaction of swingers.

Because privacy is paramount, the exact number of swingers is impossible to know. As awareness of relationship styles increases, the standard definition of intimacy for some couples no longer automatically includes the concept of monogamy. Of course, there will always be those who adamantly oppose the swinging lifestyle. The fact that the swinging population continues to grow indicates that there is some purpose or function that makes it worthwhile for couples.

In the face of this lack of hard evidence, this book arose from an actual research study to share some of the answers to the questions researchers have not asked: What is the construction of sexuality among swingers? What are the roles and rules of swingers? Why do men and women choose this lifestyle? What is considered a quality relationship by swingers? And the number one question about swinging that everyone asks, what is the difference between swinging and cheating?

To find the answers, I interviewed sixty individuals and asked a series of questions that addressed the four components of the survey: demographics, marital satisfaction, sexual satisfaction, and those questions specific to the swinger lifestyle.

Based on the results of the academic research conducted for the dissertation I completed in 2018 for my doctorate, this is what I learned: Of the sixty individuals who completed the survey, the average swinger was in his or her late thirties, Caucasian, having obtained secondary levels of education and is above average in their socioeconomic status. Swingers are also politically conservative, and employed in white-collar professional roles.

All of the research indicates that those who do participate in the swinger lifestyle are typically private, established, and otherwise ordinary people. Their overall stability is what allows them to withstand sexual arrangements that do not adhere to social sexual norms. This stability also allows them to more easily cope with secrecy, as opposed to less stable people.

Dr. Tracy Riley

In the course of this research, I gathered not only statistics, but compelling stories of unique, wonderful, and occasionally heart-wrenching experiences of real people with non-monogamy. This is one of them:

> *Stephanie became involved in the Lifestyle initially because she wanted to explore being with other women. Her partner, Nick, was in agreement and supported her desires. From there, Stephanie and Nick went on to discover full swapping activities with other couples. Stephanie admits that there are times she enjoys the Lifestyle and other times she prefers only the sexual company of Nick.*

Throughout this book, I'll share with you what I've learned, the statistics and the stories. I'll share with you the Whys, the Wherefores, and most importantly, the How-Tos of the Lifestyle. At the end, you'll be ready to redefine yourself and your sexuality, if you so choose; if you choose not to, you will have a better understanding of yourself and others. Whether you ultimately choose monogamy or consensual non-monogamy (or resolve to be an old-fashioned cheater like the hairdresser at the start of this chapter), you will know that you are making an informed decision, not merely accepting the default which society has handed you.

Interlude:
A Brief History of Swinging

Swinging--or "wife swapping" as it is sometimes called--has been the subject of experiential investigation for decades, yet there hasn't been much in the way of research done on the swinging lifestyle. Because people within the Lifestyle do not advertise their life choices, swinging has only been occasionally studied on an academic level.

In fact, the exact origins of swinging as a modern phenomenon are unknown. Some speculate that it may have begun with couples during and after the Second World War, but unfortunately, the evidence is mostly rumor.

Tradition has it that during World War II, the practice became popular among military men and their wives in California, especially among the US Army Air Forces fighter pilots, who faced the highest fatality rate of any branch of service. Some moved their wives to bases in California, but some did not. The combination of loneliness along with facing a high chance of mortality led to an unusual social scene in which non-monogamy between these pilots' wives and other pilots became acceptable. By the time the Korean War ended, these groups had spread from military bases to nearby suburbs. The media became aware of these occurrences and labeled the activity as "wife swapping."

Dr. Tracy Riley

Though the custom may have thrived in the shadows for several decades, the sexual revolution of the 1960s brought it to mainstream public awareness. The first official swinger organization, The New York City League for Sexual Freedom, was founded in 1963 by Jefferson Poland.

Its goal was to promote and conduct sexual activity among the members. A few years later, Poland moved to the San Francisco area and started the East Bay Sexual Freedom League there. In following years, Poland established various League chapters and allowed others to run them.

Because nudity and sexuality are often intertwined in the public's mind, Poland took on both taboos at once, making national headlines in August 1965, when he and two "twenty-somethings" performed a "nude wade-in" as an act of civil disobedience at a park in San Francisco. The sensational protest drew quite a large number of reporters and spectators.

The group of three swam around the bay in the park and emerged from the water, naked and holding hands. Once police arrived, Poland and his companions were immediately arrested.

As you can imagine, the event generated unprecedented interest in nude sunbathing at public beaches and recreational areas. Poland's goal was to send a message that being naked was okay, and he and his group advocated for public nudity in Golden Gate Park and in several local Bay Area beaches.

Ethical Cheating

The East Bay Sexual Freedom League sponsored a number of nude parties, which were held at private residences, where couples could attend naked and engage in sexual activities if they chose. Richard Thorne, the twenty-something African-American head of the East Bay Sexual Freedom League, wanted the parties to help participants to free themselves of guilt and shame by disallowing society to manage their sex lives.

Dr. Tracy Riley

Chapter Three
So You're Thinking about Becoming a Swinger

I once overheard a conversation in a hair salon. The stylist was telling her client about her relationship with her boyfriend. The client, knowing the stylist's marital status, asked innocently "Are you and your husband swingers?" Without missing a beat, the stylist admitted, "I'm not a swinger; I'm a cheater."

You may be wondering how you could be comfortable within the swinger lifestyle. While it may be tempting to just jump in with both feet—or both sheets, as some say—there are many things to consider. The Lifestyle requires some special skills to keep yourself and your partner happy and growing. Over time, you can develop these skills through a combination of education, conscious effort, and, yes, frequent engagement of the Lifestyle.

The skills needed to thrive in the Lifestyle can be summed up in two words: Honesty and Communication.

Honesty: the Only Policy

You may be shocked at the idea that honesty is a requirement, but that's what makes Ethical Cheating actually ethical. It's what makes the difference between swinging and cheating.

Ethical Cheating

Probably the most important aspect when considering the swinger lifestyle is to be honest: Honest with yourself and honest with your primary partner, as well as any potential partners you may consider. Honesty puts you in the position to support yourself as well as your primary partner. Honesty is the best way to navigate—no, it's the only way to navigate--this lifestyle.

(Note that due to societal pressures, you don't have to be open about your choices with your neighbors, family members, coworkers, or casual friends. Keeping secrecy for yourself and your partners is standard, and it's not what I mean when I say be honest.)

Communication: With Yourself First

If you are thinking about pursuing the Lifestyle, the first person you must be honest with is yourself.

Self-examination is vital. Being able to know why you want to experiment and perhaps engage in this decision is important. You won't have to defend your position to family members, coworkers, or neighbors, but it's important to know within yourself why you are considering this. Ask yourself: What do I expect from these experiences? What rewards can I foresee? What negative consequences am I afraid of? As you read this book and hear stories about successful swingers, you may discover both benefits to look forward to and pitfalls to avoid.

Some people explore the Lifestyle because their partner is pushing them into it. I've heard many women admit they are not interested in the Lifestyle, but they participate so that they don't have to worry about their partner becoming unfaithful. Abigail shared that she felt forced from the beginning to go along with her husband wants. Once she's in the moment, she occasionally loosens up and has fun. However, overall, she doesn't prefer the Lifestyle.

You must be clear within yourself that you're choosing to explore this lifestyle for you—because it excites you, offers opportunities for learning and growth and fun, because you want to. If you're feeling forced or coerced, resentment can easily weaken the very relationship you are seeking to honor.

Several chapters of this book will outline the "how to" of swinging. Before you can get to that, you must understand the why. I can't say that clearly or loudly enough. Going through the motions, going along with your partner, or feeling pressured to take one for the team are not good reasons to experiment with this lifestyle. It can be a rocky road. However, when navigated successfully, the rewards far outweigh the risks and negative factors.

If you didn't fully know yourself before venturing into this endeavor, you will have no choice but to get to know yourself when you do. We are all carrying around junk in our minds about sex, gender, and what's "normal." It is impossible to grow up in our culture and escape picking up puritanical and inaccurate ideas about sex. Some of our beliefs are buried so deep they can drive our behavior unconsciously, without us even knowing it. Because of these beliefs, it's common to oppress ourselves as well as others around us.

Self discovery could be an entire book all its own. Getting to truly know yourself is a constant journey. But, let's not digress. Self-discovery could be an entire book all its own. Get comfortable with the idea of being okay with your decisions—who you really are. It's hard work, yes. However, the benefit is that you become free to choose how you want to live your life, and what goes on behind closed doors is your business and perhaps that of your partner!

Once you begin to know yourself better—which has many benefits beyond facilitating swinging—you can begin to use sexual change as a path toward reprogramming yourself. Whatever your thoughts about sexuality, monogamy, and relationships, you learned them from someone--perhaps your parents, previous partners, or your culture. If you can learn those things, you can also unlearn them and relearn some new ways of thinking. Since monogamy doesn't equate to relationship satisfaction, being aware that you can explore the Lifestyle and still have a wonderful relationship is great news.

To begin to truly know yourself, get comfortable owning your feelings. Jealousy and insecurities may arise, but no one can make you feel any particular way. Be able to accept that, regardless of what your partner does with another person, the way you feel in response to that is based on you. Even if your partner wants to do something that isn't in line with your initial agreement, how you respond is up to you. (This could be its own book, and in fact, many books have been written about this topic. The sooner you make this realization, the happier you will be, whether you choose a life of consensual non-monogamy or the vows of celibate monk.)

> *Anna always wanted to be with another woman, but she wasn't sure how she felt about her husband also being with another woman. One night, while using some liquid courage, she was able to spit out her fantasy and her fears about what it meant for their relationship. Much to her surprise, her husband encouraged and supported her desires. During sex, they began to talk about it more and eventually found another female to join them in the bedroom. Anna was thrilled she was able to explore her sexuality, her husband supported her, and she worked to overcome any possible insecurities she may have had.*

Getting in touch with your feelings is harder than it sounds. When we feel bad, it can be hard to accept responsibility for how we're feeling. It would be much easier if someone else were to blame. Of course, as adults, we accept responsibility and accountability for our actions and our feelings. Or at least, we should strive to do so.

When we accept and take responsibility for our feelings, we are given choices. We can talk about how we feel, and we can choose whether or not to act on our feelings. It allows us to understand ourselves even better, and thus set our limits and boundaries that much stronger. Knowing our feelings, being able to ask for support from others, and establishing our boundaries are all great ways to improve our self-esteem and our overall quality of life. That's a lot of good stuff coming from having sex with multiple people.

Communication: Be Honest with Others

Once you've started on the path of being honest with yourself—and that's a never-ending journey on its own—and made the decision to talk to your partner about Ethical Cheating, it's vital that you learn to talk clearly and listen effectively with your primary partner and with anyone else you have sex with. In my private practice, I often start with teaching couples some basic communication techniques. Unfortunately, most people listen to respond, so they miss key aspects of what is being said. When we listen to understand, it changes the dynamics of the conversation and the outcome.

> *Leigh Anne had serious concerns about becoming involved in the Lifestyle so she came into my office to discuss her concerns before addressing them with her husband. Her husband was determined to get Leigh Anne out of her comfort zone and was being what he felt*

> *was encouraging and supporting. Leigh Anne felt pushed and coerced. After she practiced getting her thoughts into words in the office, she was able to openly communicate her feelings to her husband. Eventually, the couple did begin participating in the Lifestyle and now work with new couples to show them the ropes.*

Insecurity is inevitable within the swinger lifestyle, because swingers are human. People wonder about such questions as: What if my partner enjoys sex with someone else more than me? Can I really watch my partner having sex with someone else? Can my partner watch me without becoming jealous or upset? Being able to ask for and receive both reassurance and support is critical to making the Lifestyle work for you.

We have all felt insecure at some point and been afraid to ask for the reassurance we need. At the same time, we have been irritated when our partners didn't read our mind and just offer up the reassurance we crave. Perhaps you're thinking, "I shouldn't have to ask for reassurance," but part of being honest with yourself and others is fearlessly communicating your needs. It takes enormous courage to ask for support and to share our vulnerabilities.

Giving the same reassurance and support we seek is equally vital to lifestyle success and limiting insecurities. Be proactive in reassuring your partner of your love and affection. Put some thought into how you can let your partner know how important they are to you and how important your relationship is.

Reassurance is an important part of faithfulness. Talking about faithfulness in a book about sex with multiple partners may seem odd to you. While many people describe having sex with only one person as being faithful, it seems to me that faithfulness has very little to do with who you have sex with. Faithfulness is about honoring your obligations and respecting yourself, as well as your partner. In other words, it's being honest with yourself and others.

It's vital to take a look at what you can do to reinforce how important your primary partner is to you and vice versa. Many couples have certain activities they reserve for their primary partner: perhaps particular sexual behaviors, overnight sleepovers, terms of affection, even kissing may be reserved only for the primary partner. The rules may change over time, which is another reason communication is so vital to success.

> *Dawn and Brian started the Lifestyle with a rule of no kissing anyone else during sex. Over time, that rule didn't seem to matter as much, so they relaxed it and noticed how much better their encounters became with other partners.*

Before you and your partner can establish boundaries for the two of you as a couple, you will want to consider your own boundaries. Consider how you can communicate them clearly and stick with them without fail. It goes without saying that being able to say "no" is an important part of the Lifestyle. You must have a clear sense of your own limits and be able to push back if those limits are challenged. Knowing and ultimately respecting your limits will keep you feeling good about yourself and help prevent regret.

Some limits may be about the sexual behaviors; others may be about whom are you willing to have sex with. Are you willing to try something kinky or out of your comfort zone with a new sexual partner? Limits about safe sex and whether or not to use condoms are a must, and should definitely be included in the conversation with your primary partner.

I've often said in private practice—to everyone, not just swingers—we teach people how to treat us. As we stand up for ourselves and protect our limits and boundaries, others will learn to respect our limits and boundaries as well. Just like many of the lessons of the Lifestyle, this is something we all need to apply in many aspects of life, not just swinging.

> *Carol eventually found her voice when her husband Dan insisted they get together with a much younger couple, near the ages of their adult children: Angela and Brian. Initially Carol refused, but Dan persisted and was relentless. Carol was relatively new to the Lifestyle whereas Dan had many years of experience. He taunted her with comments like "take one for the team" and "I would do it for you."*

Carol reluctantly agreed, and they met the younger couple. During dinner, Carol privately let Dan know she was not interested in inviting the young couple back to their home, and she was furious when Dan did so anyway. The two couples took separate cars and drove the few miles to their home.

Once they arrived, Brian asked Carol some questions about her conversation with her husband during the car ride. An uncomfortable conversation ensued. Brian decided the evening was over before it got started, so he and Angela left shortly after arriving. Dan was furious with Carol, and they got into one of their worst arguments ever; their relationship was truly in jeopardy.

Carol felt disgusted, ignored, and humiliated. Dan felt he had lost the perfect opportunity to have sex with an attractive young woman half his age. It took several therapy sessions for them to see each other's perspective. Ultimately, Carol recognized the importance of setting her limits and sticking to them, no matter how much Dan insisted she waiver. The couple remained in the Lifestyle for many more years. They never had such challenges again, due to their communication, limit setting, and adherence to personal boundaries.

Defining and sticking to your own boundaries is very important. It's equally important to know and respect your partner's boundaries. Beyond that, when meeting another individual or couple for potential play activities, it's suggested that you have the conversation about their boundaries. It's much easier to know the rules before the passion and playtime begins than to be in the moment and told something is a hard no.

Being in the Lifestyle takes planning, and not just planning what will happen in the bedroom. Our time is limited, and we are busy creatures. Many of us feel that we have more commitments than we do time. Meeting other swingers, scheduling group get-togethers, going to parties, and carving out time for play, can all take a great deal of commitment. You'll have to ask yourself if it's truly worth it.

Making the Decision

Swinging isn't for the faint of heart; it takes communication, affection, faithfulness, and overcoming insecurities to be successful with the Lifestyle. You must recognize and adhere to your limits and boundaries. The swinger lifestyle takes planning and knowing yourself, being honest with yourself as well as those around you.

One couple had this to say how the Lifestyle has helped them:

> *Joining the Lifestyle has really strengthened our relationship. We're not normally social people, but we've met some amazing people that we really enjoy being around.*

So, what do you think? Is the swinger lifestyle for you? Once you dip your toe (or other body part) into the water, you may decide it's the perfect lifestyle for you. The rest of the chapters to follow are all about how to get started, what to do and what not to do, and WHO to do!

Dr. Tracy Riley

Chapter Four
The Number 1 Question. (What's the Difference Between Cheating and Swinging?)

The pain caused by cheating is real. It can leave long-lasting scars. In no way, is this book an attempt to minimize the pain of infidelity, or make light of it, or provide excuses for it. I do want to explore the differences in the Lifestyle and infidelity. One interview I did for my dissertation demonstrated that:

> *Jeremy shared that he engaged in the Lifestyle back in his mid-20s with his then girlfriend. While he admits to some intrigue and curiosity about re-engaging in the Lifestyle now, he has such difficult and uncomfortable memories of how things went. His experience left him feeling cheated on and ignored. He felt destined to remain monogamous to avoid the heartache he felt way back when. After meeting the right partner, he realized his desire to re-join the Lifestyle could be trusted with his new partner, knowing this time the experience would be mutually beneficial.*

As I said before, the title of this book is quite the oxymoron. Interestingly enough, I did receive some negative feedback about the title when it was presented to people in the Lifestyle.

They often replied:

> "Swinging is not cheating."
> "I don't like being referred to as a cheater."
> "Don't call me a cheater."
> And similar statements.

If you're in the Lifestyle, you are well aware of the fact that the swinging lifestyle, while it includes having sex with others outside of your primary relationship, does not constitute cheating. This book isn't written for the swinger; it's written for those trying to understand the Lifestyle and those who may be interested in trying out the Lifestyle.

It's a common question to ask—how does swinging differ from cheating?

If you're considering this lifestyle, you may have some questions to consider:

> "How can I cheat on my partner?"
>
> "How can my partner cheat on me?"
>
> "I hate the thought of my partner with someone else; how am I going to watch?"

After all, you've made the commitment to be exclusive and monogamous. The thought of cheating goes against your moral compass.

Dr. Tracy Riley

Here's the huge monumental difference between cheating and infidelity. Swinging situations take place *with* your partner; it's all about having fun as a couple. It's a way for the couple to expand their horizons. Couples who swing explore their sexuality and their fantasies. So, if you're partner is there, fully aware of what you're doing, AND okay with it ... Is it really cheating?

Remember, we are being ethical—we are having a conversation with our partner prior to any such "cheating" occurring. Cheating implies deceit, dishonesty, betrayal—definitely in contrast to anything ethical.

Carolyn said this about swinging:

> *We have rules that are followed when involving other couples. We swing together, and there are no secrets. Infidelity is knowingly lying to your partner and doing it behind their back. Compersion is wanting your partner to experience gratifying sexual play. We all can see what is happening, and it's fun to watch your partner give/receive pleasure. We're all present, and all of us are open about our intentions. We are all 'in the know'.*

Despite strong opposition to the act of adultery, infidelity continues to be a popular topic for couples, and a definite threat for couples. Defining and understanding adultery is the first step in preventing it—and agreeing to the swinger lifestyle is a definite way to have your cake and eat it too.

Ethical Cheating

There are multiple ways to define infidelity, and a most important consideration is how it is defined by each individual within the relationship. As a general rule, it's outlined as the violation of a couple's assumed or stated agreement concerning emotional and sexual exclusivity. Their working definition may expand beyond sexual behavior to include emotional infidelity.

Emotional infidelity involves a greater subjectivity than whether or not sexual acts were performed out of the primary relationship. Did you or your partner become emotionally attached or connected to someone else? Did you or your partner share ideas, spend time engaged in conversation, or any other intimate acts absent of sexual contact?

If you have entered your current relationship under the conventional monogamous agreement, and go outside the relationship—either emotionally or physically—without your partner knowing, I think we could all agree that is non-ethical cheating, a.k.a. infidelity. Being ethical about this lifestyle requires thought, practice, and work.

Monogamy is generally considered the global norm, and infidelity violates the commitment of monogamy to an exclusive relationship. Infidelity is fairly common, despite the majority of people expecting monogamy. Why do individuals cheat, if there is so much widespread disapproval? There are many factors to deter such behaviors, such as the moral code, religious beliefs, or agreed upon contracts or commitments to a partner. And despite knowing how much of a threat infidelity is to a relationship, individuals continue to take their chances with cheating.

Why do we cheat? The risk of infidelity is higher among individuals who are unsatisfied, not committed, or not invested in their current partner. These individuals are likely to turn to others to meet their needs for intimacy or connection, as opposed to having an open dialogue with their partners.

Research, as well as common sense, tells us that infidelity is the result of an unsatisfactory relationship that lacks fundamental strengths. Relationships that experience infidelity are lacking intimacy, novelty, passion, and sexual satisfaction. Individuals may feel dissatisfaction and hopelessness in the marriage. This level of hopelessness hinders any effort to improve the relationship, and possibly the individual believes there is a lack of vitality to the relationship.

Lack of passion can be another reason for infidelity. Once you've gotten accustomed to having sex with the same person, passion can wane a bit. There is a discrepancy between how someone feels with a long term sexual partner, compared to how they feel with a new partner. Someone who feels undesirable, uninspired, and unwanted by their spouse, can suddenly experience those missing feelings with the introduction of a new sexual partner.

As we know, the exact number of people in the swinger lifestyle is unknown, due to privacy and discretion. However, swingers are especially committed to their partners, feel a strong emotional connection, and have their intimacy needs met.

There are many reasons people cheat, and yet as you can see, engaging in the swinging lifestyle can allow you to avoid cheating, while still experiencing new sexual partners, more passion, more openness, and sexual freedom. Your partner knows you're "cheating" or in this case, having sex with other people—therefore, you are not cheating.

Jim and Denise have been together 10 years. Early on, he brought up the idea of swinging after seeing a documentary regarding it. He said this:

> *"I love and trust my partner very much. I find her to be the sexiest and most erotic woman in the world, and I love to see her satisfied. I love to see her cum. We both trust each other, and our communication is fantastic. We have great sex, but we both understand human nature and the fact that OUR great sex isn't the ONLY great sex available. We've had extracurricular sexual activity since the beginning of our relationship 10 years ago, so making the next step to full swinging really wasn't that crazy for us. And from the beginning, neither of us has been uncomfortable with it."*

Catherine said she and her husband began engaging in the Lifestyle to vary their sexual experiences:

Dr. Tracy Riley

> *"There were some things sexually that we wanted to try. My husband and I decided that trying the swinging lifestyle might be a way to explore those desires and explore some new ones. As a result, we are closer than ever—sharing our 'secret' and we couldn't be happier."*

Michael explained the difference like this:

> *"Swinging requires communication and openness. Infidelity is built on secrecy and deception, which is not part of the swinging lifestyle. Every person we have met and played with is strong in their relationship; swinging is a way to enhance the relationship. Infidelity isn't meant to enhance the relationship and inevitably hurts it."*

Sometimes the primary relationship is already "open," but one partner doesn't know it. Discovering you have been and are currently being cheated on can be utterly awful. Feelings of betrayal, lost trust, and shame are common outcomes. Our stereotypes paint the cheating partner as the villain, the greedy partner that wants to have the best of both worlds.

As a general rule, cheating is easier than ever before. Due to technology, connecting with someone is just a click or a message away. It's also easier than ever to get caught cheating, also due to technology. Evelyn said her children learned of her infidelity because of Facebook messenger. She had been communicating with her lover through the social media outlet on her phone, and

Ethical Cheating

when her children used her IPad, they realized she was still logged in there. These pre-teens read the message and showed them to their dad, effectively outing Evelyn.

Conventional therapeutic knowledge tells us that cheating is a symptom of a problem within the relationship. Improving the relationship decreases the chances of cheating or being cheating on. Perhaps this is true. Cheating is not necessarily about a failure in our relationship. And learning that your partner is cheating on you isn't an easy situation, nor a good time to discuss a swinging relationship, although it has happened. (You may recall the Chapter One example of the couple that decided to become a "thrupple" when the husband's affair was discovered. A spouse cheating doesn't often lead to a polyamorous relationship, but it does show that careful conversation with honesty can bring about positive harmony for many people.)

Adam said this about what makes extramarital sex swinging, not cheating:

> *Communication. Honesty. Trust. Agreeing to do it ahead of time and agreeing to call it off if either person becomes uncomfortable or unsatisfied with it.*

If swinging builds trust and cheating destroys it, it makes much more sense to talk to your partner about the desire to swing, instead of cheating.

Nicole didn't realize or acknowledge the fact that she was bisexual until after she was married. She began to feel like she was missing out on opportunities to experience sex with other women. She and her husband opened up their marriage and starting exploring group sex and threesomes. They realized swinging was a great way to get her sexual needs met more often. Therefore, she didn't have to sneak around or go behind her husband's back.

Diane had a similar experience of questioning her sexuality for several years prior to getting marriage. She finally got the courage to admit to her partner she was bi-curious and wanted to experiment sexually with another woman. Her partner shared his fantasies of being with two women, so they started exploring group sex and threesomes shortly after they married. After a few successful experiences, they wanted more frequent group sex, so they easily transitioned into swinging with other couples so long as the other woman was also bisexual.

In the case of both Nicole and Diane, they felt comfortable admitting to their partners their sexual desires. Instead of cheating, lying, or denying themselves, their honesty and openness allowed them to explore their desires and get their needs met. Both women report feeling even closer to their husbands, as well as having a higher overall satisfaction within their relationships.

Ethical Cheating

We all have enough common sense to know the consequences of cheating. For the most part, nothing good comes from lying, cheating and being unfaithful. What about the consequences of ethical cheating? Those consequences are considerably different and much better.

Here are some quotes from those engaged in ethical cheating:

- *Joining the Lifestyle has really strengthened our relationship. We're not normally social people but we've met some amazing people that we really enjoy being around.*
- *It has added fuel to our sex life and we cannot keep our hands off of one another especially when we have a date with a couple. It is amazing!*
- *It has increased my confidence. Our communication has greatly increased. It makes us desire each other more.*
- *The quality of my relationship has increased with the swinging lifestyle.*

Can you be ethical AND cheat? Since the Lifestyle is about openness and honesty, it stands to reason that cheating is not the same as swinging. Swingers are happy, open and honest, and they get to have lots of satisfying sex—both with their partner and others. Chances are you already know some swingers, you just don't know they are swingers.

Dr. Tracy Riley

Swingers don't advertise their sexual prowess, yet they enjoy their lifestyle to the fullest. What are you thinking? Could you see yourself engaging in this free and open way of life? Would your partner be interested in it?

Chapter Five
How to Get Started as a Swinger

Being a Swinger starts with agreements—agreements with yourself, your partner, and your lovers.

We all have agreements that dictate our behavior. Some are spoken; some are understood as simply acceptable social norms: Don't kiss the cashier at the grocery store. Don't stare at others. Don't swipe left or right if someone shows you a photo on their phone (especially if you know they are in the Lifestyle!)

People who break these unspoken rules are often considered strange, or even irrational. These values and judgments are so ingrained in us that there are times we aren't even aware of them. Such social agreements dictate how we relate to others and how we manage our relationships.

Our moral compass will drive us to make decisions, especially as it relates to the acceptable agreements we live by. Everyone has something they are morally opposed to. You may be asking yourself if swinging is morally wrong.

We all have decisions to make. Larissa was brought up in a stringent religious home. Her mother was overbearing, and her dad was her rock and foundation. Despite the rules being strict and unwavering, Larissa married early, so as to avoid the "no sex before marriage" rule her parents had bestowed upon her in the name of religion. The stress of rushing into a committed relationship just to satisfy sexual desires drove Larissa to an addiction to pain pills. Larissa has been married and divorced now 6 times. Each subsequent marriage happened shortly after meeting the next husband to be. And why did she get married so many times? Only to avoid breaking the rule of no sex before marriage. So in order to avoid breaking one rule, she did what she morally felt was the right thing to do.

Imagine all of the time and money and effort and legal issues of each divorce she went through, just to avoid breaking the rule of no sex before marriage. She engaged in many behaviors that people would feel are morally wrong, to avoid the one rule she couldn't bear to break. Her faith is important to her; however, in what other ways has she broken the bonds of her faith?

These social rules we follow always include a certain rigidity. For most people in relationships, the primary agreement is monogamy. It's not socially acceptable to admit out loud, "I really want to fuck other people." Try saying that at the next family dinner or work gathering and see what judgments and outward criticism you get. (Secretly, other people will agree and cheer you on; possibly even living vicariously through you!)

What if you're single and you want to engage in the swinger lifestyle? If you're a female (especially bisexual), you've got it made—you're considered a highly sought after "unicorn," and

Ethical Cheating

you will have as much sex as you can handle. For the men, it's much more difficult to enter the scene as a single male. Single men are a dime a dozen.

If you're single, you're allowed to be sexually promiscuous—and hopefully you are being ethical in your promiscuity. You don't have to kiss and tell, and in this case being ethical means being safe. Protect yourself, protect your sexual partners, and while you don't have to give a list of sexual partners out, don't be shy about letting others know you are sexually active with others.

Sex is natural biology, and it ranks as a basic need on our hierarchy of needs list. If you're in a committed relationship and you want monogamy, that's your decision. No one is judging you. If you're in a committed relationship and you want to explore this lifestyle, give yourself a pat on the back for being honest about your sexual desires. Most of us want to have sex-- often and with multiple people. The smart ones try swinging or an open relationship. The not-so-smart ones end up cheating on their partners. They can't face the truth, and they won't be honest. Why is cheating so prevalent, even though it typically ends in disaster? Simple—it feels good to have sex with other people.

So with all of these things running through our heads, creating our make-up and psychological profiles, how do we become okay with non-monogamy for ourselves? How do we address it with our partner? Is it okay to be non-monogamous if we are single? We essentially have our own agreements for ourselves, but in order to successfully navigate this lifestyle, we have to enter into agreements with our partner. We will talk about those at a later point.

I may have already mentioned, it's important to know the why of entering the Lifestyle. It can't be to fix a broken relationship (just as having a baby doesn't make it better). Swinging is about enhancing a relationship that's already on solid foundation. In order to have a smooth transition, you have to already be on concrete footing. Otherwise, you'll make a not-so-good relationship even worse and potentially lose it in the process.

How do you bring up the topic in your committed monogamous relationship? That can cause anxiety for sure. Of course, you can be direct--and by direct I mean give your partner a copy of this book when you finish reading it. You can be even more direct and broach the conversation.

A less direct way is to introduce the topic with media. In the research conducted for this book and the preceding dissertation, the overwhelming majority of people learned of the Lifestyle from the media. That's right, people in the media are talking about the Lifestyle: documentaries, movies, news outlets—which are all much easier to access thanks to the internet. Chances are you've seen movies that depict the swinger lifestyle, and possibly didn't even realize it. Here are just a few of the titles:

Yes, We're Open (2012): Luke and Sylvia like to think of themselves as a modern couple, defying tradition and keeping open minds; however, when they meet Ronald and Elena, a polyamorous couple, Luke and Sylvia feel challenged to become even more open, resulting in their own sexual experiments. They slowly come to question whether polyamory is something they truly desire, or simply a sexual trend they are chasing.

3some (original title *Castillos de cartón*, lit. *Cardboard Castles)' (2009)*: This is the story of three art students: Jaime and his two friends, Maria and Marcos. Jaime attempts to set up Maria and Marcos to help with the latter's impotence, but when it does not go as planned, he intervenes. The result is three-person love life.

Wanderlust (2012): Due to financial misfortunes, married couple George and Linda are forced to sell their New York flat and move down south with George's brother, who offered him a job. On the drive there, Linda asks to make a pit stop, and the couple end up at Elysium, a bed and breakfast housing a hippy commune. The couple must decide between themselves whether they would rather stay with George's narcissistic brother, or give in to the pressure of the residents of Elysium and their "free love."

Vicky Cristina Barcelona (2008): Best friends Vicky and Cristina go on vacation to Barcelona where they meet the

Dr. Tracy Riley

alluring artist Juan Antonio, who invites them on a get-away with him to Oviedo. They agree, fully aware of the sexual implications, but the sudden reappearance of Juan's violently unstable ex-wife, Maria Elena, makes them wonder if this is a relationship they really want to get involved with.

Four Lovers (original title *Aimez Qui Vous Voulez,* or *Happy Few) (2010):* There is no denying the physical attraction between Rachel and Victor, and the chemistry between Teri and Franck is also readily apparent. The fact that Rachel is married to Franck and Teri to Victor becomes a non-issue in the couples' sex lives ... for a time. As the couples' intertwined sex lives go on and their feelings become twisted, they begin to wonder which decisions from the past were the right ones.

Professor Marston and the Wonder Women (2017): William and Elizabeth Marston are university professors working to create the Lie Detector, assisted by William's student, Olive Byrne. Through the product's trials, the three learn of their attraction toward each other, and come together in a polyamorous relationship that is not approved by their community. The three become a family and their relationship and subsequent fetishes result in William creating the voluptuous, rope-bearing superheroine Wonder Woman.

Eyes Wide Shut (1999): Dr. Bill Harfard and his wife Alice enter a strange world of mystery, danger, and seduction after attending the Christmas party of one of Bill's wealthy patients. Temptation draws at them both from seemingly everywhere, and the two must attempt to sort out the differences between their physical attractions to others and the love they have for each other.

Zebra Lounge (2001): Answering an ad published in a swinger magazine, married couple Alan and Wendy meet with Jack and Louise at the Zebra Lounge, where they swap partners for the night. Alan and Wendy feel that they satisfied their need for sexual excitement, but the feeling is not mutual; Jack and Louise refuse to give up their new partners so easily.

Love (2015): American film student Murphey dated Electra, a Parisian woman, for two years, until they had a threesome with Omi, a young Danish woman, which was supposed to be no-strings-attached; however, Murphey and Electra's relationship falls apart after Murphey has sex with Omi behind her back. Eighteen months later, Murphey is living with Omi and their son, the product of their affair, out of a sense of diligence rather than love, and an anxious phone call from Electra's mother has Murphey reminiscing about the life he had with Electra before the threesome.

2+2 (2012): Married couple Diego and Emilia are surprised to learn that their friends, Richard and Betina, are swingers. Taking Betina's invitation, Diego and Emilia attend a party for swingers that eventually leads to the two couples swapping partners. But their comfortable lifestyle as swingers takes an abrupt turn when it is discovered that Emilia and Richard have been having sex in secret.

Dr. Tracy Riley

Marriage 2.0 (2015): San Fransciscan couple India and Eric explore what it means to be a millennial couple, and how to reconcile commitment and honesty with exploration and growth. The world is not the same as it was yesterday, and neither is the world of love and sex.

Real Life Wife Swap (2004): Each episode focuses on different aspects of the swinger lifestyle, from the mundane to the extravagant. Episode one is about a swinger party for a hundred guests, episode two is about the creature comforts and etiquette, and episode three is about a hotel specifically for holidaying swingers in the French Pyrenees.

An Open Invitation: A Real Swingers Party in San Francisco (2010): The couple across the hall don't exactly keep their sex lives secret, and from what others can tell, it's great; so when their neighbors, who are in a relational slump, encounter them, the couples come together and, well, it's porn, so ... pun intended.

Palm Swings (2017): When Allison and Mark move to Palm Springs and discover their neighbors are swingers, they decide to step into their world. However, swinging turns out to be a trial by fire for their marriage.

Bob & Carol & Ted & Alice (1969): Bob and Carol are taking strides to become more emotionally open, somewhat to the dismay of their more conservative friends, Ted and Alice. After each of them has an affair except for Alice, Alice demands the group have a foursome. The foursome falls flat and the film ends with the two couples departing from each other, holding hands with their original partner and staring soulfully into each other's eyes.

The Ice Storm (1997): On the Friday after Thanksgiving, two couples and their children become entangled in love affairs fueled by revenge, hatred, and mere boredom. The family members are injured by each other's infidelity and shamed by their own actions, until the death of one of the children draws them back together.

The Overnight (2015): What was supposed to be a casual night amongst friends turns into something else entirely when Alex and Emily find out that Kurt and Charlotte are swingers. With the kids in bed, the group of four become a true foursome fueled by alcohol and marijuana.

How to Plan an Orgy in a Small Town (2015): Sex columnist Cassie returns to her small hometown for her mother's funeral, bringing bad memories of being slut-shamed back to the surface. Her old neighbors resent being portrayed as bumpkins in her writings, so Cassie challenges them to host an orgy to prove they are not as backwater as she wrote them to be.

Maybe you haven't seen any of the aforementioned filmography, but I'd be willing to be you have seen at least one movie that made a subtle reference to the Lifestyle. It was the 2000 remake of the 1966 Classic Children's Book, grossing over $345 million worldwide and seen every year in December: *How the Grinch Stole Christmas.*

There's a scene when baby Grinch looks through a window at party goers throwing their car keys into a large fish bowl. This is referred to as a key party. At the end of the night, each woman chooses a random set of keys from the bowl and then spends the night with the owner of said keys.

Of course all noble swingers will tell you they don't just have sex with anyone; they are typically standards, requirements, and oh yeah—those agreements again.

We all know that the movies are not real life depictions in any area. Think of the popular Law & Order. We see a crime being committed, the investigation unfolds, and an arrest is made all within the first half. During the second half of the show, the alleged criminal is arraigned, a jury is selected, the trial is held and bam—a verdict. All of this happens within 52 minutes, plus commercials. In real life, it can take years for any one portion of the process.

As you watch any of these movies, keep in mind that your real life experience will most likely never mimic what you see. Perhaps what you watch will give you some ideas on how to proceed, meet people, or even what to say in awkward situations.

Ethical Cheating

And consider that these movies are usually made by monogamists for monogamists. Though they may offer a glimpse into the Lifestyle as a voyeuristic thrill, they often end up condemning it, acting as cautionary tales to reinforce the monogamous norms of society. Watch the movies, but take them with a grain of salt. See them for what they are—entertainment.

So, back to broaching the subject with your partner. Imagine this: If you could have one meal every day for the rest of your life what would it be? Steak? Pizza? Keep in mind it's only one meal, but it can be anything you want. After a while, it gets boring. Yes, it's good, but ... That is why people swing. They can have their main meal (anything they want), but every once in a while, they'd like to sample something different: a different flavor, extra spice, something exciting simply because it's new.

Whether you've been together for a few months or many years, the conversation to swing can be scary at first. Sex talk is a taboo for many couples. Yet having sexual fantasies involving other people besides your primary partner is perfectly normal. It's vital to know you can't force or coerce your partner into the Lifestyle—they have to go willingly.

Start with some gentle easy questions. Before introducing your ideas, ask about his/her wildest sexual fantasies. There is a good chance your partner will suggest a fantasy that includes group sex. Take advantage of that moment and move the discussion further along. If your partner asks you to also share a fantasy, share your ideas by asking questions, such as, "What do you think of a threesome, or a foursome?"

Another easy and perhaps fun way to bring it up is to during sex. Take the heat of the moment, engage in erotic sexy talk, either during foreplay or the main event.

For obvious reasons, do not bring up sex with other people right after you've had sex with your partner. The last thing you want is to give the impression that you're unhappy with the current state of affairs. Just like having a baby, swinging cannot save a struggling relationship. What it can do is ease the boredom, make your primary relationship better, improve your bond, and help you connect on a deeper level.

For men, it is important for you to know that often times, women have felt like they were coerced or forced into the Lifestyle. Please don't do that to your significant other. If you talk about it, give her ideas, and let her lead the way, it will work out way better for you in the long run. Women can have a healthy sex drive, too. After all, swinging wouldn't be nearly as much fun if that wasn't true.

The smartest approach is for the man to give the woman the control from the very beginning. Happy wife, happy life—we've all heard the phrase, and it goes for non-married partners as well.

Once the initial conversation is started, and you've covered the movies, there are other options. Playboy TV has a series called

Swing. It's arguably the most entertaining and accurate resource on swinging. This reality-style series takes place in a mansion full of swingers, and each episode features a couple who is new to the Lifestyle and wants to give swinging a try.

A quick search of the podcast app on your smart phone will deliver multiple various podcasts to listen to. *Life on the Swingset, The Curious Couple, Swingin Around, Swinging Outside the Lines, We Gotta Thing, Bliss Bringers, Swinging Downunder*—just to name a few. How's that for your listening pleasure on the morning commute?

Even if you hear "no" in the beginning, always be supportive and kind to your partner. Be kind, not pushy. It may take some time for your partner to think about it and get curious and consider it in the future. The best way to make a decision is to have a great deal of information.

Swinging is fun and something couples do together. Otherwise it's cheating, and there are no ethics involved in infidelity. Above all, keep your partner's desires and their needs as the priority. The Lifestyle has to be congruent with the quality of your relationship. Lots of communication, checking in with your partner, and oh yeah—those agreements again.

Let's get back to the agreements that are a huge part of the Lifestyle. There are many rules, agreements, and considerations to make before you get into the Lifestyle. If you haven't talked to other swingers, there are many things you might not even think about until there you are. You definitely want to know your boundaries, limits, and ideas prior to dropping your britches.

Start with deciding where you will engage in the experiences. Is your home an option, and if so, what about your bedroom? Some couples decide their bedroom is a sacred place where others aren't allowed. Others feel that they are already comfortable there, so the more the merrier.

Are you interested in the full sexual exchange with others, or soft swap only? Soft swap typically means anything that isn't genital penetration. What about voyeurism? Do you let others watch you, but not join in? Do you want to just watch other people, but no touching allowed?

The majority of couples engage in the same room, but what about being in a separate room? Some individuals have said they prefer to be in a separate room, because they can't concentrate or focus on their swinging partner with their primary partner (spouse) right there in the same room.

Do you plan to, or is it okay to, swing separately? Will you take a "don't ask, don't tell" approach and do your own thing, or notify your partner before you go have solo sex.

Are condoms required?

Is kissing allowed? This can be a lengthy and ongoing topic of conversation. Some people believe kissing is the most intimate act of sex and therefore only reserve it for their primary partner. Others feel that kissing can really get the passion going and it's a great way to get something started with a new partner.

What happens when the two of you meet another couple, and three of you are totally in sync, but that fourth person is a little weird, out there, or just plain gross to their counterpart? Do you take one for the team and do it anyway?

Are you looking for bisexual females, bisexual men, or bi-curious couples?

Are you willing to go outside of your race for a swinging experience? Perhaps you wouldn't consider dating or marrying outside the race, but will you have sex with someone of a different race?

What are your age requirements? What is too young, too old?

Will you set a limit for alcohol?

Will you set a limit for recreational drugs?

Will you give out your real names, or try on alter egos with different names?

Should you give out your real phone number or use a private app to communicate so no identifying information can be garnered?

Dr. Tracy Riley

When you post photos on a profile, or send them to another couple, will you show your face right away or wait until they ask?

Some couples won't engage in repeat play with an individual or another couple, within a certain time frame. It could be one month, six months, or even a year. Some will only play with a couple once. This is to avoid any potential emotional connections. And it may also be to have as much variety as possible.

Who will do the communicating? In order to avoid secrets and surprises, couples will need to decide on how to handle the communications. Some people love the flirting that takes place before a meet up. Other people find that it causes trouble. One option is no solo chats, always communicating in a group text.

The most highly sought after phenomena is the Unicorn, as they can be lots of fun. Single ladies that swing are in high demand. Unicorns can also have their own set of requirements to ensure their safety and protection; these will be different than the requirements of couples.

Will you put a limit on your drinking for your encounters? Relying too much on liquid courage isn't healthy in any situation. In the case of swinging, it may contribute to you accidentally breaking some of your agreements.

Ethical Cheating

These are the kinds of things you will want to discuss with your partner, once you decide you want to give swinging a go, and before you start meeting other singles or couples. Like any good rule book, it is bound to change over time, and you can always add or take away rules as your comfort level grows.

As rudimentary as it sounds, consider writing down your agreements, and make sure each partner has a copy. You might also want to review them from time to time and change things. It can also be fun to see where you started and how far you've come and how much has changed since the beginning. It's kind of like a sexual time capsule, if you will.

There is an appendix in this book, with an outline of the agreements to consider.

In the upcoming chapters, we will discuss where to find swingers, how to meet up with couples, and how to go to your first sex party. I've heard many people suggest they don't have a good enough body, or they're too insecure, or they fear jealousy. Keep reading: There is much to learn about how easy it is to overcome those things.

Dr. Tracy Riley

Chapter Six
How to Meet Other Swingers

So, if you're this far into reading Ethical Cheating, you must be still considering this lifestyle. Admittedly, it's not for everyone. Those that can and do take the plunge report feeling happier, freer, and much more sexually satisfied as a result of this choice. Maybe you've read this far and you're still thinking there's no way it would work for you. That's okay, too. Education is one of the most important factors in everything we do; whether it's buying a car, building a home, or making any other large purchase—we have to educate ourselves as much as possible. Consider this some good learning and a fun read. (Pardon the Alabama slang there—you can't take the Alabama out of this girl).

Where would you possibly meet swingers? The quickest and easiest way to find out about local clubs, parties and events is through the Internet. There are plenty of websites that offer an outlet for meeting others.

Websites

Here are ten websites to get you started.

www.adultfriendfinder.com

Adult FriendFinder is everything you would find in a

traditional dating site, but with many more features and filters. Whether you're looking for a relationship, an extra partner for you and your significant other, or just a casual fling, AFF has you covered. Are you LGBTQ+? Are you into BDSM? Are you just interested in learning more about alternative forms of sex and dating? AFF is your go-to.

www.swapfinder.com

Swap Finder is a site for swingers who are looking for anything from additional partners, to virtual experiences in mutual masturbation, to friends to share interests with. SF features two-way webcam video chatting, instant messaging, and forums for sharing knowledge and experiences. There are also features that help people get to know each other better before meeting up in person, providing safety on top of fun.

www.swingerdatelink.com

SwingerDateLink is another site for swingers that has a lot of free features, such as free video and text chat. While joining is free, some features are exclusively for Premium members, such as certain search filters. Premium users also have the option to only allow other Premium users to find them, to ensure that they only receive serious inquiries. The site has a small but dedicated user base.

Dr. Tracy Riley

www.sdc.com

Swingers Date Club (SDC) is unique in that it hosts swinger events, both public and invite-only, to help people who have met online engage in-person in a safe environment. As a member you can also use the site's vacation booking feature to plan a sex-centric vacation for yourself, you and your partner, or a group. SDC is LGBTQ+-friendly and open to any relationship style, as it promotes itself as offering resources in educating its users on their sexuality, relationships, and health.

www.swinglifestyle.com

Swing Lifestyle is one of the more highly-praised websites for swingers due to its usefulness as a directory, even though most of SL's features are locked behind a paywall. It has a calendar of events, a long list of recommended products and resources, a booking feature for swinger vacations, and more. Those looking to promote their swinger-adjacent services can even become an affiliate with SL. Whether you're looking for a partner or a quality lube, you can find what you need here.

www.intothelifestyle.com

Into The Lifestyle verifies all of its members, not just paid users, to prevent catfishing and bot spam. Members have access to photos, videos, blogs, podcasts, and events through the website, alongside its social-networking features. It has a matching feature similar to other dating apps, but it's more

Ethical Cheating

notable for its dedicated forums on specific topics, such as blogs exclusively for wives, or for those looking to practice tantric sex.

www.swingular.com

Swingular offers its users extremely detailed personal profiles to ensure matches are made as closely as possible. These filters allow users to not only match by sexual preference, but also by kinks, fetishes, and specific sex acts, including whether they like to be on the giving or receiving end, so very little is left to guesswork. This site even has a feature specifically for booty calls that's just as detailed. Any way you swing, you can find your match on Swingular.

www.kasidie.com

Kasidie supports anonymity, unlike most others of its ilk. Much of the site is free and open to the public, so participation is very much at the user's own risk. Club listings, secret community meetings, parties and events, and much more are supported by Kasidie, and emailing and friending other members is completely free. Access to the instant messaging feature, as well as the site's archive of porn and podcasts, requires a paid membership.

www.quiver.us

Quiver.us (not .com) boasts a ton of success stories for its users who have found partners that fit their lifestyle. The website is easy to use, making meeting and befriending other members a simple and streamlined process. The site hosts a directory for swinger events and locales, and it allows users to filter who is able to see their profile, ensuring no one undesirable can contact them.

www.swingerzonecentral.com

Swinger Zone Central offers most of its site's features to members for free at the cost of not having as many features and filters as other sites of its kind. Features include the ability to see which users viewed your profile, instant messaging, forums, blogs, video chatting, and event hosting. It also has an online store for sex toys and products, and if you do pay for a membership, you are able to browse anonymously.

All of these are very similar to traditional dating websites that cater to singles looking to find a more monogamous relationship.

Once you decide you are ready to meet other swingers, this is the easiest and fastest way to meet like minded people. You may decide to stick to one website, or you may choose to create accounts for several of them. Following the website prompts, you'll create a profile, which in this case may feel like a lot like placing an advertisement that you are available for sex.

Placing the ad or creating the profile isn't complicated. Be sure to decide in advance what you want to say about yourselves. You

Ethical Cheating

may look at other profiles to get an idea of what to include. Most importantly, after you've met a few couples, you may feel the need to go back and revise the profile to include things you didn't think about the first time around.

> *Emily let her husband create the profile for the two of them. After a few dates, when her husband had been offered the opportunity to "pay for play", Emily went back and redefined their profile to include they didn't play separately and they weren't interested in paying for sex. They learned that just like a using a traditional dating website, you have to be specific as to what you are looking for.*

Including some photos is important. Just like you want to know what your potential matches look like, they want to see you as well. It's easy enough to use photos where you black out or fuzz up the face. That's fine in the beginning of conversations with someone. Once you exchange some emails, you'll want to show yourself.

But wait, what if it's my neighbor, or my kid's teacher, or a member of my church? Well ... that means they are also looking for sex through a website designed for that very thing. They are also expecting discretion and privacy.

When Emily updated their profile, she also made mention of that fact that she knew all men looking to hook up had a penis, and she didn't need to see a photo of it as proof. It's common for at least some of the photos to include pictures of genitalia. Don't be offended by it. Even if you are just meeting someone for sex, most people want to see faces and bodies—they assume the genitals are present.

Many times, couple profiles are saturated with photos of the woman alone with only one or two featuring the man, or perhaps it's the other way around. Make sure your profile includes photos of each of you, showing off your personality. Both of you will be joining in, so photos of both of you are important. You are looking for a four-way connection, and it can be complicated and take some effort on your part.

What do you say when you contact someone whose profile you find appealing? Be simple and straightforward. You are all on the website for the same reason, presumably. They know why you are reaching out. Tell them your ages, your interests, and maybe how long you've been in the Lifestyle. This is especially important if you are brand new to the Lifestyle. You might want to mention where you live, as in the city or a general area of town. One paragraph is sufficient—don't give a life story or bombard them with tons of emails and questions.

If they respond—great. If they don't, move on to the next profile that piques your interest. Swinging is incredibly similar to dating. You are not going to click with everyone you meet—but there is an important difference to keep in mind: you aren't going to marry them. You may have wonderful sex. You may become great friends for life, or you may never see them again. Either way, know that expectation almost always outweighs reality.

Out of 166 people asked, over 75% of them reported meeting other swingers through Internet swinger websites, so we know it works.

Swinger Clubs

In some metropolitan areas, there are swing clubs. Again, a quick search of the Internet will lead you in the right direction. Even if you don't live in a large city, chances are you aren't too far away from one. Swinger clubs vary from city to city and state to state. Typically, there are some similarities. There is a party/club atmosphere, and it's usually dark and anonymous. It's easy to hang back and observe without the expectation of joining in.

Many swing clubs expect you to join as a member. This is a formality, so the establishment can say it's a private, member's-only kind of place. Some will require your legal name as a member, yet once you walk in it's fine to give any name you choose. One such couple always went by Nancy and Drew at clubs and parties. Admission fees vary, and usually only cash is accepted. It may be a "bring your own snacks" place, or they may have food and drinks available, or it could be a little of both.

Most clubs, especially the good ones, will have some sort of security guard walking around. Not necessarily a uniformed officer, but just a few people focused on making sure everyone is safe and protected. Think hall monitors from junior high school.

You may want to go early, right as they are opening. This is when things are more relaxed, so there isn't much playtime happening, and you can mingle. Or you can go a couple of hours after they open, when the action is taking place. Some clubs do not allow you to come in and immediately get naked. You have to wait until the appropriate time when play is allowed.

There will be several semi-private rooms, usually with seating for the voyeurs to watch. Each room may have a different theme. There might be BDSM rooms, glory holes, fantasy play (think gynecologist office, workout room, fetish play). You may find an area for rope play, massage tables, even dancer poles and lots of loud music.

Be sure to take it all in and stick around to check it out thoroughly. You probably paid a hefty entrance fee, so you might as well get your money's worth.

Private Swinger Parties

Private swinger parties are typically invitation-only gatherings held at someone's home or a hotel suite. There is usually an entrance fee for couples and single men. Some parties deny

Ethical Cheating

entrance to single men, and typically single women are allowed in free of charge. You may be asked to bring an appetizer or food item—think potluck meal.

As with anything, there aren't many hard and fast rules about private swinger parties. There may be a theme—think 80s, Grease Night, Back to School, Mardi Gras themes. Dressing up in costume can be great fun and a good way to get conversation going once you arrive.

Definitely plan on bringing your own adult beverages, and whatever you do—don't sit it down and leave your drink unattended. Although most swingers are good people committed to consensual interactions, predators have been known to take advantage of the sexually-charged setting and atmosphere of anonymity to target swinger parties as hunting grounds, sometimes slipping date-rape drugs into drinks. It's a good idea to bring your own cup with a lid.

How do you find out about swinger parties? You may find them on the Internet websites as an upcoming event. You will probably hear about them from other swingers. Over time and through experience and research, you'll know which ones are more in line with your type of party. Some parties are exclusively 40 and under, while other ones may include walkers, wheelchairs, and oxygen tanks. (True story).

No matter where you choose to meet fun sexy people to get naked with, be sure to plan, plan, plan. Bring condoms—and now is not the time to discuss safe sex, so just do it. Bring lubrication, sex toys, lingerie, change of clothes, even some toiletry items in case you are in need of a shower (before or after the fun—maybe even during?)

Finally, be sure that you are welcome:

> *Jill and her husband Tommy were invited to their first swinger party right after Christmas. As it turned out, Elliot had invited Sue, who had invited Nelly, who had invited Autumn, who invited Jill. Jill and Tommy were relatively new to the Lifestyle and had never been to a private party. Once they all arrived, the hosts of the party, Bryan and Jenny, were not exactly thrilled to have that many extra people attending—without invitations!*

Clothing Optional Resorts

This may not be where the beginner swinger gets started, but it could be. Many swingers also like to be naked in public—but it's not a requirement. When you hear the phrase "clothing optional", you may think of either a sun-soaked orgy, or a piece of old, worn-out shoe leather. Truth be told, neither portrayal is all that accurate.

There's a lot to love about clothing optional resorts—the sexy atmosphere, the ability to sunbathe naked, and the fun entertainment. As expected, there are a wide variety of options, from luxurious resorts to the mid-range or value options.

Ethical Cheating

You'll find them spread throughout the world and be sure to do your research. Some are couples only, no singles allowed. There are a variety of experiences and activities. Some have public sex opportunities, and others are quite discrete as to when and where the play time happens.

Swinger Cruises

Though they are not quite as prevalent and accessible as the resorts, there are a handful of large swinger cruises each year, ranging from 1000 to 2000 couples. Some are full take-overs, and the others are only half take-overs, which means vanilla people are on board, and possibly some children. Some are marketed as a swinger's cruise, and others a little more discrete in their advertising. These cruises are definitely not kid-friendly, but sometimes families travel together.

The atmosphere is sleek and sexy, and you're joining other passengers who are ready to mingle and get naked. With that many people on board, you are bound to find someone that piques your interest (and that of your partner).

Bars are open later, orgies are elective, and hand sanitizer is heavily encouraged. You can be sexy, flirtatious, and join in or watch from afar or even up close. Be sure to bring a card with contact information and even a photo of you and your partner to give out.

Dr. Tracy Riley

Social Media

There are many more swingers on social media than you can imagine. After all, swingers are regular people, and they do regular things—like have social media profiles. Swingers have found ways to set up private anonymous social media profiles. There are secret communities where they can interact daily with other couples. If you consider using any social media platform, be sure to fully understand the security features—you don't want to be found out through social media.

As you can see, there are plenty of places, ways, and opportunities to meet other people who want to have sex—even those that want to have sex with you! It's common to be nervous at first, and even nervous at every first meeting. The benefits far outweigh the risks, and by reading this book, you clearly have a desire to take the first steps.

What are you waiting for? The right time? There is no such thing. Just jump in and do it. You probably have a few stories of some first dates that didn't work out so well. You will definitely have some stories to share as a result of being in this lifestyle. I can't wait to hear them, and I'm always listening. Let me know how well you did.

Chapter Seven
The Green-Eyed Monster of Jealousy

> *Let jealousy be your teacher. Jealousy can lead you to the very places where you most need healing. It can be your guide into your own dark side and show you the way to total self-realization. Jealousy can teach you how to live in peace with yourself and with the whole world if you let it.*
>
> —Deborah Anapol, *Love Without Limits*

Swinging is what you make it. It's about letting go of outdated notions of sex, relationships, and what is "normal." Can you do that? Can you let go of hang-ups and allow yourself to be completely free while allowing your partner to do the same?

"But, but, what about JEALOUSY?"

Jealousy can be a true obstacle to this way of life. It feels rotten; most of us will do whatever it takes to avoid feeling it. In an ideal world, there would be no jealousy. We could all love and have sex without restrictions, without expectations, without the green-eyed monster rearing its ugly head.

But, since we are all human, jealousy is going to happen at some point. And it's possible it will happen around something that you weren't even expecting to be an issue.

Dr. Tracy Riley

> *Patrick and Susan had been in the Lifestyle and had a couple they saw regularly for full swap/same room. There had never been any issues regarding jealousy until one particular night. Susan and the other husband finished up first and were making their way out of the room. She heard the other wife, in the heat of passion, moan out Patrick's name. It made Susan so jealous she couldn't see straight. As a result, she and Patrick never played with the other couple again.*
>
> *Susan was as shocked at herself as she was upset with the other wife. It seemed so innocent and natural to moan out a lover's name, but that was her husband's name being called out. She felt like her husband could be enjoyed by someone else, but calling out his name was something only she was allowed to do.*

You have to be both strong and self-aware if you are going into this lifestyle. We all have our pet peeves, even if we don't know what those are until they happen. Swinging can bring out the best in you, and it can also bring out the worst. Be sure to continuously engage in self-assessment to keep yourself in check.

Zach had this to stay about jealousy:

> *I used to think we got jealous in the Lifestyle, then we played with a couple that got mad at each other about their emoji use with us when we chatted. Like, really??*

We all just fucked each other and emojis is going to be your issue?? I don't believe my wife and I were ever that bad, and we handled our shit appropriately. Jealousy very rarely pops up now, and when it does, we talk like adults.

Men—take note here. Do not get into the Lifestyle thinking you can have all the sex you want, with whomever you choose. Many men go into the Lifestyle with the preconceived notion it's sex all the time. What men don't always know, especially in the beginning, is that the woman is in charge of how this process goes.

Many men are not only unaware that the woman is in charge, they are also unable to handle it. They see their woman out at parties or clubs, getting hit on like the lady of the hour, and they may feel left out, vulnerable, and of course jealous. They see their lovers having fun and if they focus on it too much, it becomes an ugly scene.

Women call the shots. Men have to wait for the woman to give the indication that it's time to play, or which partners to play with. The sooner and better the man realizes this, the better off the night, and the Lifestyle for that matter, will progress.

The Lifestyle doesn't breed jealousy—jealousy exists in many places. We are human after all. Many people mistakenly think that monogamy is the antidote for jealousy; it is not. We have all experienced jealousy with a monogamous partner that is kept away from us for some reason. Perhaps work, guys' night out for football, or any other reason prevents our partner from having full on focus on us, and we begin to feel envious or a little green-eyed. Jealousy is an emotion we all have to deal with at some point—whether we are participating in the Lifestyle or not.

Jealousy in and of itself is not one emotion, but rather a multitude of emotions, under one umbrella. It can show up as grief, rage, hatred, or self-loathing. Perhaps it is an expression of insecurity, a fear of rejection, or a fear of abandonment. We may feel jealous if we feel left out, somehow feel inadequate, or not good enough. Jealousy is a mask for inner conflict—a conflict that is crying out and desperate to be heard and responded to.

Because jealousy is ingrained so deeply, it can be difficult to recognize it in the moment. We go to great lengths to avoid feeling it. Or worse, we project the negative emotions associated with it onto our partner. Projection is a defense mechanism that involves moving a painful emotion outside of ourselves to someone else—someone we are especially close with.

Some jealousies are based on being territorial—something is mine and I want everyone to know that. Yet here you are about to let someone else have what is yours—for at least a brief time period. While sex makes us feel powerful, it also opens up our vulnerabilities. The combination of being vulnerable along with territorial can be a disaster in the making.

Ethical Cheating

Stan had this to say about jealousy:

> *Jealousy was never an issue for me. I love seeing my wife get fucked by other guys. It's hot, and it turns me on so I never felt jealous. If she's having a very good time, I'm super happy about it. I don't feel jealous because I have an amazing marriage, amazing three kids, amazing home. I don't fear losing it because I know my wife loves the marriage and family that we have. She nor I are looking to jeopardize something good. I don't feel insecure by another guy because there's always going to be a guy fitter than I am, with a bigger dick than I have, and if she's enjoying that dick, great.*
>
> *My wife has never exhibited jealousy either. As she knows for me, when we have sex with other couples it's just a moment for me to have a good time and good pussy and that's it.*
>
> *In the end it's all about having a good time and fun and when it's over, we go back to our regular life.*

Jealousy can be a major problem in any relationship, but the way of the swinging lifestyle can bring it into sharp focus. Jealousy has been linked to low self-esteem, and feelings of insecurity and possessiveness. Neuroticism—a general tendency to be moody, anxious, and unstable can also lead to bouts of jealousy. Feelings of inadequacy in your relationship and an over-dependence on your partner can be the demise of any relationship, monogamous or not.

Again, taking a personal inventory to enhance self-awareness is vital to the Lifestyle. Not everyone can handle it. There is good news though. If you recognize yourself in any of this, then you can unlearn jealousy. You can decide you are strong enough to look jealousy square in the face and tell it to move on! Once you acknowledge the underlying emotion, you can position yourself to do some healing.

Take a class, join a group, find a good therapist, practice meditation—go to work on yourself first, before venturing into the Lifestyle. This may mean healing old wounds, opening up to new possibilities, or gaining health and freedom from fear. And the best part—somewhere in the midst of all of these wonderful things, you can also gain sexual freedom.

Linda had this to say about jealousy:

> *It's human nature to be jealous. There is nothing wrong with it, the only thing is how you handle it and how you communicate with your partner. If you didn't get a little jealous every now and then, even if it's extremely minor and fades quickly, then maybe you should look at your relationship.*

The fear of being sexually inadequate can be a secret wound that you aren't aware of. Keep in mind, sexual achievement is not measurable. We cannot measure ourselves on some ranking system—and why would we want to? Eventually and hopefully you will begin to take notice of so many different people's way of expressing their sexuality, you will stop comparing yourself to others. You'll begin to enjoy each experience for what it is: unique, engaging, fun. Great lovers are not born—they are made by variety, repetition, and a zest for sex.

> *Rhonda shared that for her, it feels as if jealousy has been replaced with awe and pride when she sees her partner with someone else. She knows no one would ever be able to take her place, and she is confident in her partner's feelings as well. She believes jealousy is not an emotion that proves your love and connection.*

You don't know what you don't know. Buddhists call this beginner's mind. It's okay to make mistakes—in fact, you have no choice but to make mistakes, because you don't know what you don't know. So be graceful with yourself. The test comes in being able to create within you a strong basis of security at your core, a security that is not reliant upon being sexually exclusive or owning your partner.

You'll revel in being able to grasp your personal power, while learning to understand and love yourself without the need for someone else to endorse you. Self-esteem comes from within—not from another person, situation, sexual encounter, career, or family. Once you recognize that, you are free to give validation to yourself because you don't need it from others to know how

Dr. Tracy Riley

truly amazing you are.

> *I notice that jealousy comes and goes, depending on how good I feel about myself. When I'm not taking care of getting what I want, it's easy to get jealous and think that someone else is getting what I am not. I need to remember that it's my job to get my needs met. I feel the jealousy, but I'm not willing to act on it, so it mostly goes away.*
>
> Barbara from *The Ethical Slut*

Once you have decided not to act on feelings of jealousy, they lose their hold over you. You can begin by reducing the amount of power jealousy exerts over you. How do you do this? Allow yourself to feel it, even though you won't like it, and it may be painful. Feel it anyway—don't push it away. Ask yourself some questions:

1. What emotions am I really feeling at this moment that make up the feeling of jealousy?
2. What does my jealousy show me about myself?
3. What else is going on in my life that could be a contributing factor?
4. Am I taking care of myself properly?
5. What is going right in my life right now? Make a list of the positive aspects in as much detail as possible.

Once you have taken the time to ask yourself these questions by way of self-assessment, you're still not done. Knowing the answers is a great start, but there's more. Find someone you trust to discuss the feeling with. Communication is an important key to overcoming all of the feelings associated with jealousy. It can be done, and it will happen less frequently the more you are able to openly address it.

The person you discuss jealousy with may or may not be your partner. In an ideal relationship involving perfect people, it would be your partner, but no one is perfect, so it may be better to talk to someone more impartial or experienced, whether a professional counselor or a friendly confidant. The important thing is that you discuss it with someone who understands your lifestyle choice and will refrain from judging it. Many monogamists will simply justify your feelings of jealousy rather than help you deal with them.

It's important to own your jealousy. If you try and pretend that you aren't jealous when you are, people will see right through you. They may consider you dishonest or to be trying to manipulate situations. Neither of those are ethical. If we don't acknowledge our emotions, they have a way of getting our attention one way or another. It could come as intense rage, irrational anger, severe anxiety, tantrums, or even physical illness that pops up out of the blue.

You can feel jealousy without acting on it in a negative way. This is big step is taking away the power of the jealousy. Feel it, acknowledge it, and give honor to your feelings. That may seem like a weird process to something that feels so yucky, but it works. The more you do it, the easier it becomes. Of course, for most people, jealousy subsides over time as you become aware of the Lifestyle, your boundaries and agreements, and how to move forward. Be good to yourself. Love yourself wholly and thoroughly. Learn to reflect on your strengths.

The most important part of love is when someone sees us at our worst, sees our weaknesses, our imperfections, and our smallness—and still loves us anyway. We have to practice loving ourselves in the same way. You don't stop loving your partner because they do something stupid, so love yourself in the same way.

A simple poll on www.reddit.com yielded the following breakdown with 330 votes.

- 43   I used to get jealous in the Lifestyle, but now I don't
- 118   Jealousy was never an issue for me.
- 30   Jealousy continues to be an issue on a regular basis.
- 139   Jealousy creeps up every so often.

As you can see, jealousy is a common situation that can happen whether you are a part of a monogamous relationship or the more open swinger lifestyle. So, don't avoid the Lifestyle simply because you are worried about jealousy. It happens to the best of us.

Ethical Cheating

Striving to overcome jealousy doesn't mean it will magically disappear. Chances are good that you have already experienced it in your relationship, and chances are good that you will definitely experience it within the swinger lifestyle. Don't throw in the towel at the first sign of jealousy. Recognize the feelings, make a self-assessment, and don't try to ignore them. Jealousy is quite subjective and can be different each time you experience it. The most significant aspect is to identify it, understand it, communicate about it, and then evolve to lessen it.

Jealousy and all of the thoughts and feelings that go along with it are just a little speed-bump or hurdle along the way to sexual freedom, happiness, and lots of sex! You've got this, you can do it. The question is, do you want to?

Dr. Tracy Riley

Chapter Eight
Logistics: The Nitty Gritty of Getting Down and Dirty

We have covered a great deal of material so far. You know what swinging is, and you probably have a pretty good idea of whether or not you'd like to give it a go. You have learned some new ideas on how to communicate with your partner about it, how to get started, and even how to meet other swingers. You already know you can't avoid jealousy, so you know how to handle jealousy when it comes up.

Now we can talk about the logistics of swinging. Some things you may not know or haven't thought of until you are in the moment--and then ooops! What do I do now? How do I proceed? This chapter will give you some additional how-to information you might want to know ... just in case.

In case you are still in the decision-making process, let's recap some questions to ask yourself:

- Why do I want to be a swinger?
- What are the benefits?
- What are the drawbacks?
- What are my expectations? My partner's expectations?
- How is my current relationships? Do I really believe

my relationship can withstand this?
- Am I choosing this or is my partner pushing me?
- Do I think it's wrong?
- How do I feel about my family, friends, neighbors and co-workers finding out?
- Have I discussed the agreements with my partner?

Swinging is not a question of right or wrong. The real question is this: Is it right or wrong for you? The more you know, the more you can accurately answer that question. There are many things to consider within the Lifestyle—and you aren't the only factor. Your partner isn't the only factor. There is more. So much more.

Once you've arrived at the decision that it's right for you, there are some real-life logistics to deal with:

Fake People

One of the biggest complaints about the Lifestyle is the large number of fake accounts, fake profiles, and fake people one encounters online. This is a form of trickery called "catfishing." The majority of the fakers are actually single men, pretending to be a part of a couple. They do this because they want your photos. They may want to meet, coming up with some "reason" why the female counterpart is unavailable, but "she's fine if I meet without her."

Dr. Tracy Riley

How will you know if a "couple" is really a single man? When you begin chatting with someone online, ask for a current photo of the two of them. You may even go as far as to ask them to hold up a peace sign or make a funny face so you know it's a current photo. Typically, the single male posing as a couple won't answer questions, will ask for more than one photo, and the "female" is never available to chat, or take a phone call, or send a photo when you ask for one. She's at work, she's with her family, or she's taking care of the kids. You'll start to get suspicious and when you press for details, you won't get them.

It might be harsh to call these people scammers—they are usually harmless and just want a collection of photos for personal titillation. They won't waste anything but your time. Eventually, they will lose interest and move on to another couple for a fresh start.

Even some couples—who may or may not be one person pretending to be a couple—are not really interested in meeting up. Rather, they get their kicks with exchanging dirty emails and photos. That's okay if they are honest about that from the beginning. Of course, they usually aren't, and you may think you're getting closer to actually meeting, and the truth is they have no intentions of meeting you.

This is disappointing and annoying, but sadly it goes with the territory. As monogamists say, "Before you find your prince, you might have to kiss a few frogs."

Ethical Cheating

Expenses

Whether you go to a private party, meet another couple face to face, or go to a club, there are expenses you may not be expecting. Depending on where you live and where you are going, travel costs may be minimal, or you may find yourself traveling hundreds of miles to meet up. Other travel costs can include hotels or resorts, plane tickets, and car rental.

Of course when you meet your swinger couple, you don't want to meet up at a fast food place, right? Most swingers meet in nicer, more upscale, restaurants. Drinks and appetizers can be costly.

At a party or a club, there will be entrance fees, typically cash-only. Parking can be a cost, depending on where you are going. Some private parties don't allow parking on their street, in which case couples are required to park at a nearby public area and take an Uber or Lyft to the main event.

Don't forget the cost of condoms, hygiene products, and birth control.

Of course, personal care may not be considered exactly a swinger cost, but manicures, pedicures, beauty treatments, costumes, and clothing can all add up.

If you have small children, you'll need a babysitter.

Unless you are so financially well-off that it isn't a concern, you may consider starting a swing fund to put away a few dollars each week. Just be aware that swinging costs money, and be prepared – or recognize that now isn't the time to use discretionary income on this lifestyle.

> *Paul and Abby had just began dating and immediately went into the Lifestyle together. Abby started noticing how often Paul picked up the tab for everything when they went out with other swingers. It made her uncomfortable, and she noticed there were times when it appeared to make the other couple uncomfortable as well. She also noticed out of five or six meetings—at nice restaurants with drinks, appetizers and a few meals—no one had ever offered to pick up their tab. The costs added up quickly. Abby pointed this out to Paul, and he stopped offering. Whether the server asks how to split the checks or not, Abby and Paul started taking the initiative to ask for two checks.*

Dating

You may have figured it out by now, but swinging is a lot like dating. That is essentially what you are doing. You can't expect to click with everyone you meet. You won't like everyone, and not everyone will like you. Hard to believe, right?

On the other hand, don't be overly picky. You aren't looking to marry another couple, and most people are not perfect. Keep an eye out for major red flags though. People who post pictures that are 5, 10, even 15 years earlier are usually trying to hide their age. You won't know this until you meet them.

> *Gabrielle went with her husband Steve to meet Max and Lucy. Max and Lucy's profile stated they were both 40 years old. Through conversation, they mentioned their grandchildren and their ages being 9 and 10. Gabrielle did the math in her head quickly and realized there was no way their ages were correct. When (gently) confronted, Max and Lucy admitted they had lied on their profile to attract a younger group of potential couples.*

Just like when you're dating, expect to be nervous. If you don't click with a couple, no big deal. Just move on to another couple. Give yourself permission to take it slow. You don't have to have sex on the first date. There is no reward for speeding through this process.

If this lifestyle is right for you, you will find many opportunities to make it work for you.

Pick a location you are comfortable with: perhaps a local bar or restaurant. Be sure to know the atmosphere. Going to a place with very loud live music makes it difficult to have conversation to get to know someone. If you're trying to keep your lifestyle a secret, returning to the same restaurant on a regular basis might tip off the wait staff.

The most important thing is to be yourself. After the introduction, then what? If there is natural chemistry, you won't search much for things to talk about. Talking about experiences in the Lifestyle is always an easy go to. If you don't have experiences to talk about, that's fine too. You can share that your new to the Lifestyle, and maybe learn from a more experienced couple.

Be sure to have an exit strategy in mind, in case it's not going well, and you really want to get out of there. Something as simple "I have to get up early for work tomorrow" will suffice. You're all adults, and they may figure it out. If they ask to meet again, and they just aren't your cup of tea, be polite. The swinger crowd is quite small, and you don't want to get a reputation for being abrupt or rude. Many times, people just make tentative plans and don't get back to you. Have a response ready, and even rehearse it ahead of time: "We would love to be friends with you guys and see where it goes." That sounds just like something you may hear on a traditional date, right?

Initiating the First Step

Just like dating in the traditional means, going on a swinger date is much the same. They are interviewing you, and you are essentially interviewing them. Whether or not you specify "we're here to fuck," it's a given and understood.

Be yourself, be friendly and open, look your best. Like meeting anyone new, what do you talk about? Well, hopefully the topic of swinging comes up. At this point, it's at least the one known thing you have in common. That's why you're there: to talk about sex and to have sex. Most of the time, it's a great opener for conversation that can take the edge off.

It might be helpful to keep in mind, most likely they are as nervous as you are. You may have a tentative plan to play on the first date, but don't hold fast to the plan. Be flexible. It's good to take the time to get to know someone. But don't let the opportunity slip away due to anxiety or nervousness. It takes quite a good bit of planning to make any meeting happen, so it's always good to be prepared to take advantage of an opportunity that pops up.

How will you know they are interested and how will you let them know you are interested? Simple. Communication. You all know why you are there; it's no secret. After all, chances are you met on a dating app for swingers. Just ask "Do you guys want to come back to our place, get a hotel room, or go to your place?" Whatever applies, just ask. If you don't ask, the answer is always no.

Once in the private space, any number of possibilities will present themselves. A little alcohol never hurt, but too much alcohol can lead to performance issues as well as compromised judgment.

Opinions vary when it comes to recreational drugs. Some people say that while they may be a part of recreational life for you, you should refrain during your first encounters with others. Too much alcohol and drugs can lead to bad decisions and later regret. Other people believe that whatever you're comfortable with is what you should do. You have to decide for yourself in the agreements you create for both you and your partner.

What if we get stood up?

This happens quite frequently with two-on-two personal meetings. You could be getting ready to walk out the door when you get a text that reads, "something came up," and your plans are moot. Even worse, maybe you have traveled a great distance to get somewhere, and the plans are canceled just as you're arriving in town. Next to people not looking like their profile pictures, this is probably the most common complaint.

People flake out, and they cancel with total disregard to others. No one likes it. Chances are you will never know the real reason. The truth is most likely that they changed their minds—simple as that. It's also likely you won't hear from them again.

What happens if you are the ones that have to cancel? Sometimes, there are legitimate reasons—things *do* come up last minute. Don't send a text or email. That's too easy. Take the time to make a personal call to explain the situation, apologize, and ask to reschedule.

Swapping

There are different levels of swapping. There is soft swap—where the main event is left for your partner, but all ways of foreplay lead up to that. It can be fun and a good start to working up the courage to fully swap partners.

It's up to you and your partner to decide what you want out of the Lifestyle. There is no right or wrong, only what is right or wrong for you (and your partner).

Some couples never even soft swap, and they watch others and do their own thing in the company of others. Every couple is different, so it's always advisable to ask what the rules are. Everybody's rules are different, and you can't possibly keep up with what everyone is okay with. Don't worry about asking again; they probably forgot they've already told you.

Same Room or Separate Room?

One of the most common questions that comes up within the swinger discussion is *same room or different room?* This "rule" also varies, based on personal preferences. The overwhelming majority of couples stick to same room. They like to watch their partner getting into the action and enjoying themselves.

Angelica and Doug admitted they preferred separate rooms, but nearby. They liked to hear each other from afar. Once they got home, they would have grudge sex, role playing that they were mad at each other because of the "cheating."

Dr. Tracy Riley

This is another one of those question to ask early on. Make sure you and your partner are on the same page so that you agree upon where you will partake in the act. Also, when meeting a new couple, be sure to ask about their preferences. Make sure their plan is compatible with yours.

Dress to Impress

Whether you are going to a club, a party, or just a two on two date, be sure to dress the part. Take the time to do your hair and makeup (females). Men will want to be well groomed. If you want to be a successful swinger and have the best time, put effort into your appearance. You don't have to have professional hair and makeup, or wear a formal gown, but play the part.

This isn't a ballgame, so flip flops, tank tops and ball caps are out—even in Florida. Most people will only give you one shot at a first impression--so if it doesn't impress, you're automatically crossed off the list. Is it fair? Maybe not. But it happens. Put your best foot forward.

Condoms

This is one of those topics about which you will find a great deal of discussions and debate. "No glove, no love" is a common motto when it comes to engaging in safe sex. Others will say that they get tested every few months, so there is no need to protect themselves or their sexual partners. Getting tested for sexually transmitted diseases is highly recommended and important. However, you don't know whether or not you will get an infection two days after your last test, and then infect multiple partners before your next test, so condoms are always a good idea.

Some people will use condoms with new partners, and refrain from using with partners they are familiar with. There is not necessarily right or wrong, but a matter for you and your partner(s) to discuss and agree upon.

Depending on where you go, condoms may be required and even provided. At some clubs or parties, it's common to see reminders to use them. Upon signing in, you may have to verbally agree or agree in writing that you are aware of the condom use policy.

Other places, such as private parties or with your own endeavors, you'll want to consider if they are right for you.

Flying Solo

Most couples swing together, but what happens when you want to go at it without your partner? That goes back to your agreements. As long as your partner is in agreement and is aware of your activities, it's ethical, and therefore not cheating. It becomes cheating when your partner doesn't know your intentions, and you are hiding things.

What If Things Go Right?

You will gain a wonderful sense of freedom once you have some solid swinger experiences under your belt. You'll discover you can handle swinging, that it's fun and you like it! You can feel proud of yourself for getting over insecurities and working through jealousy. What a sense of relief! We all know that sex is a great stress relief. So more sex is more stress relief, right?

How do you know you've made it there? You may find yourself smiling more, feeling happier for no particular reason. You and your partner are having mind-blowing sex. You look forward to the next adventure. You are taking better care of yourself. You're even considering sexual adventures you haven't tried before: girl on girl, group sex, BDSM, or other kinks.

As you can see, this chapter covered a lot of those little nitty gritty things that you just don't know until you're there in the moment. These things can easily be overlooked or forgotten because you don't know what you don't know.

No two situations are ever the same. Even if you are playing with the same couple at the same location, whether it be a party, a club, or a private residence, the dynamics change regularly, just like they would if you were on a traditional date with a relatively new partner. Have fun with it. What you do behind closed doors is no one else's business. You are an adult, you are allowed to do adult things—like having meaningless sex with your friends.

Chapter Nine
Stories, Experiences, and the Real Dirt

Throughout this book, I have shared countless stories of real people who live the Lifestyle. There is no one-size-fits-all approach to this way of living. There is only the size that fits for you. As you can imagine, all of the identifying names and contact information have been changed to protect privacy. Once you have stories of your own, please let me know so I can share them with others—protecting your privacy as well.

The stories, experiences, and real dirt listed in this chapter came from multiple sources. Some of it is anonymous, and some of it came to me through various websites and blogs. The bulk of it is drawn from personal interviews I conducted with participants within the Lifestyle.

I have included the questions I asked before each section. Responses have been edited slightly for clarity, but profanity and obscenity have been left in.

Have You Had an Experience that Turned You Away from Swinging?

Spouse Tried to Initiate Meetup Without my Knowledge Husband and I have been married nearly 20 years. We had one extremely brief conversation last year that included if either would be interested in a threesome. We both agreed that it was intriguing, but I included that it can be very tricky if there isn't full trust in the relationship or communication. It was left at that. Earlier this year, we had a vacation planned in the early spring that ended up being canceled. In the meantime, I came across a notification email that he had tried to find a swinger couple to meet up with during this vacation. Nothing became of it—obviously—because the trip was canceled, but I was upset because it was done behind my back. If he had asked beforehand, and it didn't come as such a surprise, I might have gone along with it. He said he was only curious to see if someone responded. More recently, I discovered chats with a swinger couple. The chats (that I know of) were just questions about the Lifestyle, but then I found out he sent this couple a very private picture of me that was only meant for the two of us. I was furious and humiliated. His response was that he got off showing someone else a picture of me that he thought was sexy. Once again, if he had asked beforehand and it didn't come as such a surprise, I might have gone along with it. I feel blindsided, humiliated and violated. – Ellen

What are Your Frustrations Within the Lifestyle?

Finding 100% compatible couples can be surprisingly hard. There is almost always an imbalance. Soooo many men posing as couples or being overly aggressive. –Bonnie

Worst thing about the Lifestyle: People we've met and others we've worked to avoid. I don't know if it's more than real life but there are some fucked-up people in the Lifestyle. Most are just in this for themselves, and with that comes a lot of lies like telling you what you want to hear. We've worked tirelessly to avoid couples who don't care about safety or privacy, and that's kind of a full time job in the Lifestyle if you care about that. We listen to the rumors, we do our homework, and we move cautiously. –Benjamin

We didn't understand how much work it would be to continually articulate what we were thinking and feeling about certain experiences, so we could progress without hurt feelings. Some people immediately jump to things like full swap and separate dating and are totally chill, but we had to work at it. –Oliver

Be cautious of couples who get into the Lifestyle to "fix" their issues. If they are having marital problems, the Lifestyle more than likely won't help, and then you can get caught up in the drama. I had many great experiences; I have fulfilled about every fantasy I could have imagined. The bad was seeing swinging couples/friends that you get close to, having their marriages go bad. But that could have happened regardless of the Lifestyle. –Lucas

It's not for everyone. However, having three gorgeous, fit, energetic, and experimental women all to myself for a weekend was great. Also my wife's and my marriage is better than ever and better than we dreamt of. –Will

Dr. Tracy Riley

It's an amazing feeling to have great sex with new and attractive party people. However, I get frustrated about the cavalier attitude about condoms and safe sex: "I get tested every three months." Good, but so what? You still raw dogging it. Hubby and I met up with a couple whose long-term girlfriend had cervical cancer. He refused to use condoms. I laughed at him because I thought he was joking. He wasn't. They were both 40—so old enough to know better. And I wasn't about to educate them on that so the only answer was to flee as fast as possible. –Abby

What are Some Great Benefits to the Lifestyle?

The best thing about swinging is that even if it sucks or doesn't work well, you still have your partner to turn to and hang out with. And it's amazing with the two of you, so if the other person / couple / sex doesn't work you'll still have a grand time. –Sophia

When it is Good, it is Great!.

My wife and I had a threesome last night with another guy. I've been getting a bit tired from all the chatting, and dealing with ghosts and shit-talkers. Made me question if it is worth the effort. I'm bi and enjoy expressing that with my wife, and she loves to be shared. People talk about a single woman being unicorns, but finding a guy who we are both attracted to, who can communicate, who doesn't ghost or is just pic hunting, and can perform is not as easy as people make out to be. Sure, there are more guys getting around, but the list quickly narrows.

So we met this guy online, exchanged pictures, chatted easily, and made plans; he turned up on time and with good hygiene, made good talk, was respectful, and played to our tempo, but at the same time gave my wife (and me) an amazing time. It seems worth it again. It was so much fun sharing her with someone who was able to read the room and give us what we were after. Sigh --Mason

Our Neighbors are Swingers

We've been chatting with a couple for a few months now. Due to work rosters, we'd been unable to arrange a meet. Very early on we'd discovered we lived in the same suburb. No big deal. Anyway, last night we finally arranged a meet. Dinner and drinks at a local club. Nothing too fancy, just something informal and pressure-free. Due to the other couple being new and cautious, we hadn't exchanged face pics. So we arrive first. Five minutes later they walk in, and lo and behold, it's our neighbors. Across the street and one down. We'd never spoken but wave when driving past or bringing the bins in. Turns out they're an awesome couple, very easy to talk to and quite attractive, so who knows where things end up. –James

Do Key Parties Really Exist?

You've seen references to key parties in the movies, and it's somewhat of a common thought pattern for swingers. Does it

Dr. Tracy Riley

really exist? Would you consider going to one, or even hosting one?

We have been swinging for many years and never seen a key party. –Jeffrey

We were at a party and talked about doing a key party. One girl was on her period and another only played with girls and there was a single guy to throw things even more off balance. It sounds like a kind of fun idea if you had the right group, but I think realities rarely match with the legend. –Alexander

I hope not! I don't want a random partner. –Belinda

We have seen it once almost as you would imagine it, but there is a very common soft version of it.

The soft version: you give everyone a playing card, and they have to find the person with the same one. Or you give men a lock and women a key, and they have to find who can open what. It's done at meet and greets, or house parties, to get people to talk to each other. No play is mandatory.

The real version: we went to a small house party in an apartment with just one bedroom, so people had to take turns to play with a time limit of 20 minutes. So the host put everyone's name on pieces of paper. If you wanted to play with a random person, you just put your name in a hat. Then anyone could draw you and you went to play.

Out of 7-8 couples maybe 10 people threw their name into the hat. One woman put her name back into the hat after each play and fucked every guy. When my hubby played with her, she complained that she only came three times and wanted to continue, but hubby wanted to respect the time limit to be fair to everyone. Her husband was "not feeling well" and didn't play at all. They are now divorced. –Angela

More a Hollywood thing and less of a real thing. Some swingers have done it after seeing it in a movie, but it's not very common. We tend to like new things and experimenting so novelties like this do happen, but it is not the regular experience. –Ava

Swingers want to pick their own partners. They want to ensure they have a physical (and often also social) connection with their partners. With a key party or randomly picking people to pair up inside a closet for 7 minutes of heaven or another similar type of game, it takes the choice out of the hands of the swingers. – Elizabeth

What Do I Need to Know as a Beginner?

It's very much like learning to walk, ride a bicycle, drive a car, playing a musical instrument: practice, practice practice! –Bud

First FMF went great

.My girlfriend (21F) and I (21M) have been talking about having a threesome for almost a year (been together for two), and looking actively for about three months. We had trouble finding a third, and we didn't know how to advertise. We were hanging out with a female friend who had us over to her house, and it happened! My girlfriend and I had been joking about doing it with this individual since we'd planned to hang out with her, but neither of us thought it was actually going to happen. We each drank a couple ciders, my girlfriend and I tried dabs for the first time, and before I knew it we were all spooning on the couch. I knew it was going to happen when they started playing with each other's hair. We ended up staying for a few hours, having sex and fooling around. I expected it to be at least a little awkward or strange, but it went great! All parties enjoyed themselves immensely, interestingly enough the third said she was straight, but very much enjoyed doing things with both of us. We all cuddled and talked after, and it was all around an amazing experience. We are very excited to do it again! We're not sure if we want to do it with the same person again, so we'll see where that goes. --Samuel

What is your Position on Condoms?

No glove, no love. Condoms are often a source of debate for any situation to avoid pregnancy and sexually transmitted diseases. In the Lifestyle, there are mostly two sides: Do or do not.

All condoms suck, in my opinion. But ... they feel much better than an STD or a pregnancy scare! –Anthony

I didn't even realize this was a thing until almost too late. I was so glad the other couple brought plenty of extras. –Leo

Whatever brand condom you decide on, make sure you train with them. Yes, you read that right: condom training. The Lifestyle presents enough new challenges. Don't let the strange-but-long-ago-familiar feeling of wearing condoms be one of them. And definitely look into MyOne Condoms. You'll definitely find the perfect fit! --Perry

Start practicing at home now! Seriously. Masturbate with a condom. Practice putting one on in the heat of the moment. Get used to fucking with a condom. Practice makes perfect. As for brands, we always make sure we have a variety of condoms my wife prefers in different sizes. It should be about the ladies. Also, make sure you have both latex and non-latex varieties due to allergies and appropriate water-based lube on-hand. –Jesse

How does Divorce Interact with the Lifestyle?

In the end, the only thing that held my marriage together was the Lifestyle. Because of the Lifestyle, my marriage stayed intact for another 5 or 6 years. Ultimately, the divorce wasn't because of the Lifestyle, but because of drifting apart and a lack of communication. –Traci

I always told my husband that at some point, I would want to get out of the Lifestyle. He acted like he acknowledged my feelings, but when it came time for us to get out of the Lifestyle, he refused. I still wouldn't say it's the Lifestyle that caused our divorce. It was the fact that he was selfish, couldn't see things from perspective, and had to have his way. Not just around the Lifestyle, but around every aspect of our lives. – Sara

I could go on and on, but I think you get the point. There are a variety of topics, conversations, and information you can gather from anywhere, so hopefully this condensed version helps give you fresh perspective on this potential way of life for you.

Real life stories from real life people sharing their personal experiences, these different perspectives of this sexy lifestyle allow you to learn from the best. There are hundreds, if not thousands of ways to spice up your relationship and/or sex life. Some of these stories may have intrigued you, and others may have left you wanting to know more. There are more stories where these came from. Swingers are often happy to talk to you, albeit anonymously at times. Nobody really wants grandma to know.

Chapter Ten
Wrapping It Up

Most likely you've been monogamous by default, thinking in monogamous terms even since childhood. Non-monogamy seems forbidden and somehow wrong. And when right or wrong is the only option you have, you may find it hard to believe you can have a healthy primary relationship and simultaneously be non-monogamous.

Let's continue to explore these ideas though. There are many ways to love, to relate to others, to express yourself, and to be open sexually. We can experience our lives in any way we choose to. And regardless of what options we pick, none of them will reduce or invalidate the other ways, nor will they diminish the love that you have to give to one primary partner. So allow yourself to open up your mind, create your own rules, and be sexually free.

Three cheers for the sexually open couple (or individual). Even if you decide swinging isn't for you, you did it! You looked at the swinging lifestyle with an open mind, gathered additional information and made an informed decision. Don't fear! Monogamy will continue to thrive and be the norm as it always has, a seamlessly effective decision for those who choose it. No one judges you for monogamy, and hopefully you aren't judging those who choose non-monogamy.

Dr. Tracy Riley

Up to eight million people in the United States are engaged in the Lifestyle, so that figure alone will let you know that it's working for some people. Well, maybe more than some people. In the first chapter, I asked you to describe your typical swinger. I wonder how your perception of that person may have changed. Do you now see a swinger when you look in the mirror?

Should you decide the swinging lifestyle is right up your alley, consider it as the development of advanced sexuality—where we all become more natural, more open, and more human. Think of sex as a physical manifestation of some things that have no bodily actuality: feelings like love and joy and happiness, emotions that go beyond surface level, intense intimacy, powerful connection, and even a level of spirituality. Allow this utopia of good things to be an honored tool to explore and discover things about yourself.

Perhaps your swinger encounters are just that—single encounters, never to be repeated. You can set up your experiences so they are "one and done." Many people prefer that--a never ending series of one-night stands. Or maybe you just teased someone and left them wanting more. Maybe you did things with your partner, while making strong eye contact with another individual or couple nearby. Perhaps you had sex with someone and you didn't even ask their name?

At parties or clubs, you could peep into a glory hole. You could even participate in said glory hole. Maybe after a little liquid

Ethical Cheating

courage, you danced naked in a roomful of people, and they were watching you—watching you with no judgment, just encouragement and fascination.

> *Stella went to a Grease-themed swinger party once, wearing a one-piece dress with a thick felt poodle skirt. The host's air conditioning had gone out a few hours before the party, and the hosts didn't have time to notify everyone. Dozens if not hundreds of people were there. And the heat was sweltering. Stella decided it was too hot for that cute dress, so she walked around in her bra and panties (matching of course). She kept on her bobby socks and black Mary Jane shoes. And(GASP), she didn't have the perfect Barbie body, and yet she relished being cooler and more comfortable than she would have been wearing the dress. That's not exactly the kind of things you can do at the work event or a family reunion.*

Imagine a world in which you have an abundance of friends, and you have sex with those friends. Many couples have been known to vacation with their swinging partners, enjoying friendships outside of sexual activities. In this busy and sometimes scary world, having an abundance of close friends doesn't seem like a bad thing.

If you choose to keep your business behind closed doors, that doesn't equal shame, for there is no shame in being open and wanting to have sex with people you choose. Society wants to dictate our norms, but how great would it be if we could live in a world where no on suffers from shame for their desires, or embarrassment for their dreams?

Have you considered the benefits that can be gained from swinging? After all, we do live in a pros-and-cons society. Many people report that the swinging lifestyle has enhanced their self-image and amplified their confidence as a sexual creature. The interviewees also stated their improved self-esteem carried over to nonsexual conditions, indicating that they were more content with themselves and their lives overall. Sexual satisfaction, friendship, self-confidence, freedom and experience are often observed as the favorable effects of the Lifestyle. Did I mention higher quantity of sex as well?

Both men and women enjoy being wanted and desired by someone other than their partner. Swinging couples have long reported their marriage or committed relationship has been reinforced as a result of their fun times. Other benefits include fulfilling sexual fantasies—and who doesn't want more of that?

Of course there is the flip side of that coin, with some negatives to the Lifestyle. One of the most common fears of swingers is that their swinging lifestyle will be found out by their "vanilla" or non-swinger friends and family. Naturally, people are worried about being exposed, judged, or criticized. The majority of people will live two lives, and the one behind closed doors is certainly acceptable to those that also participate in that lifestyle.

Here's the best part of the Lifestyle. Once you start, you can also leave it at any time. If it begins causing more stress than fun, then just stop it. If for some reason, swinging is causing problems with your relationship, or you just don't want to anymore, then just don't do it anymore. Swinging is something to do with your partner, and as long as it's going well, enjoy it. It's like any activity couples engage in together: going to the movies, taking vacations, or working out together. It's just more fun.

At some point, you may consider a break. If you find yourself having relationship issues, or work stress, or family commitments, it's easy enough to take a break from meeting other couples for a period of time. No one will judge you. There is no reward for pushing through "just because."

If your partner asks you to get out of the Lifestyle, then by all means, stop immediately. Your primary relationship comes first, and it's vital to make that your first priority. Focus on your relationship and maintaining the great communication that it took to get into the Lifestyle in the first place.

> *Ashley went into the Lifestyle, fully knowing that she wanted her primary relationship to be the focus. Ashley and Stan began the Lifestyle within weeks of dating. Because of Stan's impotence issues, he felt like he was giving her the best of both worlds. After a few years, Ashley was done with the Lifestyle and didn't care about*

Dr. Tracy Riley

> *any impotence issues. Stan insisted they stay in the Lifestyle anyway. He had improved his health to the point his impotence had improved, and he felt like it was time for him "to get his." His insistence became pushing, and ultimately Ashley had enough and she left. Their relationship didn't make it.*

It's rare that the Lifestyle itself will cause a couple to end their relationship. It's always something else. Lack of communication, absence of common interests, differing views on child-rearing are just some of reasons that relationships don't work out. The Lifestyle may have been a part of the relationship, but rarely is it the cause of the breakdown.

Since we're considering our hopes and dreams for the future—let's include abundant sex! How great would it be to have that world where no one is limited by societal rules that dictate who and when and how often they have sex. We hope someday for a world where you are the only person voting on your life's choices (and okay, maybe your partner gets a say-so).

Most importantly, after whatever swinging event you participated in, you went home with that one person—the one you are committed to living your life with, and that person is committed to you. You feel asleep with your partner, and nothing is more intimate than actually sleeping with someone next to you, as that is when we are the most vulnerable. And you chose this person to do that with—that's way more important than who

Ethical Cheating

you choose to get naked and roll around with.

By now, you've learned the ins and outs of swinging, at least as much as can be learned from a book. I trust it was informative, caused laughter, and even allowed you some reflection. You've probably reached a decision as to whether it's right for you and your significant other to give it a go. Remember, you can always change your mind! If you go for it, and you don't like it, you don't have to continue to participate. One of the best and worst parts about the Lifestyle is that no two parties/clubs/experiences are the same, even when the same individuals are involved.

While there are many benefits that can strengthen a relationship, I hope in the end that you will do (or not do) it for you—because you deserve to be happy. Whatever happiness means to you. Enjoy it, Embrace it, and Relish it in your Life—after all, it is YOUR life to live!

Appendix: Agreements

Use the following list as talking points for how you want your experiences to go. Keep in mind, these agreements may change over time. To be sure you and your partner are on the same page, jot down notes and have everything in writing.

- Start with your why. Why are you exploring the swinger lifestyle?

- Where will the experiences take place? Is your bedroom off limits?

- Full swap? Soft swap only? Voyeurism only?

- Same room or different room?

- Will you play separately or always together?

- Are condoms required?

- Is kissing allowed?

- Will you take one for the team? Will one partner ever "sit this one out"?

- Are you looking for bisexual females, bisexual men, or bi-curious couples?

- Are you willing to go outside of your race for a swinging experience?

Ethical Cheating

- What are your age requirements? What is too young, too old?
- Will you set a limit for alcohol?
- Will you set a limit for recreational drugs?
- Will you give out your real names, or try on alter egos with different names?
- Should you give out your real phone number or use a private app to communicate so no identifying information can be garnered?
- When you post photos on a profile, or send them to another couple, will you show your face right away or wait until they ask?
- Will you limit the number of encounters with an individual or couple?
- Who will do the communicating?

This will get you started with making decisions on how to proceed within the lifestyle. Feel free to add to it, based on your own preferences.

Dr. Tracy Riley

You are Invited!

Dr. Tracy Riley is available for counseling, conversation, and continuing education for your group.

Visit her website at www.tracyriley.com or call (904) 704-2527 to book her today.

Check out her other books: https://www.tracyriley.com/books

Your Call to Action

Thank you for reading Ethical Cheating: Exploring the Swinger Lifestyle!

I greatly appreciate all of your feedback, and I love hearing what you have to say—especially your titillating stories!

Your input helps to make the next version of this book and future projects even better.

Please share a thoughtful 5 star review on Amazon letting me know how much you enjoyed the book.

Thank you so much.

Check out my other books: https://www.tracyriley.com/books

– Dr. Tracy Riley

www.ingramcontent.com/pod-product-compliance
Lightning Source LLC
Chambersburg PA
CBHW031120080526
44587CB00011B/1051